D1454710

Forms of public address

THE BOBBS-MERRILL SERIES IN *Speech Communication*

RUSSEL R. WINDES, *Editor*
Queens College of the City University of New York

ROBERT G. KING

Bronx Community College of
The City University of New York

Forms of public address

The Bobbs-Merrill Company, Inc.

INDIANAPOLIS · NEW YORK

To Myrtle Embry

Editor's foreword

Research in speech and communication has created a pedagogical problem for instructors of the basic courses in the discipline. When traditional rhetoric provided esoteric theory for often esoteric courses in public speaking, a clear relation existed between the best thought in the discipline and the simplifications of the classroom. As communication research and theory has become increasingly important, however, the instructor has felt the urge to transmogrify himself into a professor of communication theory. Given the limitations of time inherent to the college curriculum, the instructor has often been forced to choose between a traditional course in speaking and a course in the theory of speech communication. This dilemma might be resolved by reserving theory courses for more advanced students and performance courses for the beginner; for some the honey, for others the wax. One might hope, however, that neither student nor teacher can accept this class approach to knowledge. An alternative is to present the traditional approach in course reading and more recent material in additional reading, lectures and class discussions. Given this strategy, a need is created for a short, comprehensive and easily digested treatment on the nature of public address. Professor King's book meets this need.

The basic premise of this book is that different forms of public discourse can best be learned through prescription and example. The

v

basic divisions are provided by the forms themselves: to influence, to inspire, to entertain. Each type is further divided, discussed under the headings of purpose, occasion, preparation and audience adaptation. Each general prescription is concluded with an example of the form and questions to help the student with his own analysis. Such a book, taken in conjunction with the presentations of recent rhetoricians and communication theorists, should provide the undergraduate with a balanced view of communication as both an academic discipline and a skill.

Russel R. Windes

Contents

Preface

Men speak in public on many kinds of occasions and for many different purposes. It is the intent of this book to classify the major types of public address in terms of rhetorical purpose and occasion; to explain the characteristics and distinctives of each type with regard to preparation, adaptation, and presentation; and to illustrate each type of address with a specimen speech.

This book is not primarily a collection of speeches. The specimen speeches are included to help make clear the material presented in the text; the text material is not presented just to illuminate the specific addresses found in the book. The specimen speeches are examples to be analyzed by the student, not models to be imitated by him. No speech and no speaker can provide a perfect model, but they can provide insights when studied in terms of established criteria.

The goal of this book is to assist students who wish to be effective and responsible public communicators. To that end, I have written as directly and simply as I can.

I am indebted, of course, to many persons who, directly and indirectly, assisted in the writing of this book. I particularly want to express my gratitude to Dr. Wilbur E. Gilman, Mrs. Eleanor M. DiMichael, Dr. Russel R. Windes, Mr. Ronald Stark, Mr. Randall Nolte, Miss Ann Jones, Mrs. William Rauth, and Mrs. Roy Kempf.

Forms of public address

ONE

The role of public address in contemporary society

The nature of public address

Public address is a dialogue between a speaker and an audience. Unless there is heckling, the speaker does all the talking, but he does not do all the communicating. The audience responds to what he says and does and conveys that response to him if he is perceptive enough to note it. A dialogue is two-way communication, with both sides sending messages back and forth. Public address does not involve one sender and a set of receivers; both speaker and listeners are sending and receiving signals; there is, or should be, reciprocal stimulation.

What takes place when a person gets up before a group to "give a speech"? What is involved in this particular kind of communication situation? A human being, stimulated by his experience and analysis, is transmitting a message in coded symbols to listeners who receive and decode the symbols, interpret the message, and respond mentally and physically in terms of their own experiences and attitudes.

To analyze what occurs, we must give some attention to the speaker (the sending unit); his motivation, intent, or purpose; the message he wishes to transmit; the symbols of language into which he encodes the message; the means or media he uses in transmission (vocal

1

utterance and visible action); the environment in which the communication takes place; and the hearers to whom the message is being sent (the receiving unit). We must also keep in mind that when the receivers respond, they transmit messages back to the speaker, so they become senders and the speaker becomes a receiver. Public address is circular communication; it is, as we have said, a dialogue. We are concerned with: who, why, what, how, when and where, and to whom.

Who: the speaker

When you speak in public, you are engaged in three kinds of activity. Vocal activity, making noises with your speaking apparatus, is one obvious element. Physical activity, the use of your body to convey meaning, is another. But these two forms of activity should be preceded and accompanied by an even more important activity: mental activity! As John Mason Brown has observed, a speaker should not appear to be the product of a marriage between a phonograph and a windmill, nor should he be, to misuse Shakespeare, "full of sound and fury, signifying nothing."

You should not be surprised that your instructors in courses in public address are concerned with far more than how you sound and how you look when presenting the speech. They are interested in all the elements of the entire communication situation. Your method of transmission is but one aspect of speechmaking. Indeed, if your ideas are worthwhile enough, they may come through to an audience in spite of your delivery, but the most polished presentation cannot make superficial thoughts profound, illogical reasoning valid, or inaccurate information true. Fluency is no substitute for facts, and poise is no replacement for preparation!

The speaker owes it to himself and his audience to have something to say and to say it as well as he can, to be thoroughly informed and carefully prepared, and to hold himself to high standards of honesty and responsibility.

Why: the purpose

There are an infinite number of specific purposes for which men speak; goals or ends vary with each speaker and every occasion on which he addresses an audience. General purposes, however, are usually listed as four: to inform, to persuade, to inspire, and to entertain.

We are analyzing purposes, then, in terms of the general response you want to elicit from your listeners. When you speak to inform, you want your hearers to understand what you say. You hope to make material clear and interesting to them. When you speak to persuade, you want your audience to agree with you or act in accordance with your point of view. You hope to influence its belief or behavior in some way. When you speak to inspire, you want your audience to feel deeply about something or someone. You hope to stir its emotions. In a speech to entertain, you expect the response of amusement and enjoyment. That response may be indicated by laughter or it may not, but you hope to please and delight the audience through your speaking.

A separate chapter will be devoted to each of these general ends, and these purposes will be related to specific occasions on which they are usually employed.

What: the subject

The "subject," as each of us learned in elementary school, is "what we talk about." In public address, the subject is that one idea on which you focus attention for the entire speech, the one concept that is central to the whole address. That topic should be significant, timely or timeless, and appropriate. You should never get up before a group to speak unless you have something worthwhile to talk about; the topic should be of contemporary interest; and you should choose subjects that are suitable for you personally, your purpose, your audience, and the occasion.

How: the methods of transmission

We code our ideas into symbols called words and transmit these words by voice and visible action. The way a person puts words together is called style, and his manner of transmitting them is called delivery. Your style depends on your choice of words; your delivery depends upon variation of the aspects of voice (loudness, rate, pitch, and quality), your manner of producing the sounds of the language (enunciation), your selection of sounds and stressing of syllables (pronunciation), your use of various melody patterns (intonation), and your use of bodily activity (facial expression, stance, movement, and gesture).

When and where: the occasion

Speech-making is done in a variety of circumstances, and the environment is an important consideration in communication. On what kinds of occasions do men gather to hear speeches? The ancient Greeks listed three: deliberative occasions, such as the public assemblies; forensic occasions, connected with courts of law; and ceremonial occasions, such as anniversaries and dedications. Although modern usage is not uniform, I have divided occasions as follows: professional occasions, on which the gathering is related to some vocation; deliberative occasions, on which men gather to discuss or debate policy; ceremonial occasions, on which men meet to observe one of the ceremonies of life; and social occasions, on which folks gather for fellowship and conviviality.

To whom: the audience

The object of every public address is to obtain a response from a group of listeners. The message is transmitted to an audience—to a particular audience. It is **for** it and **to** it, not just **before** it, that the speaker talks! If he is to be effective in achieving his purpose, the speaker must analyze the audience and adapt his message to its distinctive character.

Each audience must be analyzed in terms of homogeneity and heterogeneity. The speaker must determine what relevant characteristics the listeners have in common and in what ways they are diverse.

Homogeneity. The first task in audience analysis is discovering commonalities. In what ways are all the members of the audience alike? What attributes do they all share?

Age. If the members of the audience are all of the same age, you must adapt your vocabulary in terms of their experience and your content in terms of their interests. You would not discuss the topic of "Leisure" with the Golden Years Club in the same manner you would use to discuss it with Troop 169 of the Boy Scouts of America. But in both instances, the age range of the audience would be an important factor in your adaptation.

Sex. If you have an all male audience, you would likely choose illustrations, language, and appeals suited to masculine tastes. On the other hand, you would have to adapt your speech—even if it were on the same topic—if you were presenting it to the Lynchville Ladies' Garden Club.

Race. That all the members of a given audience may be of one race is usually irrelevant, but at times an audience may be most conscious of belonging to one racial group or another. If race was a factor in drawing the audience together, if it is clear that the group has a sense of racial identity, then you must take this common bond into account in your preparation.

Religion. Many speakers are called upon to address groups made up almost entirely, if not completely, of adherents of the same religion. When you are called upon to speak to a church youth group, or to Hillel, or to a chapter of Protestants and Others United, or to the convention of Catholic War Veterans, you must know and understand the beliefs and practices your listeners share. John Kennedy, addressing a group of Protestant ministers in Texas, spoke sincerely and directly to their common interests and beliefs. And he took into account not only their faith but their fears. Go thou and do likewise.

Organization. Often an audience will be made up of members of one organization. All the listeners may be members of the same political party, the same fraternity, or the same club. The speaker, then, must adapt his message to these group loyalties. You might easily give speeches attacking the draft to both the Young Americans for Freedom and the War Resisters League, but you should adjust your appeals and your supporting materials in terms of the organizations, their beliefs and their programs.

Community. If all members of the audience are from the same community, you can assume they will have some information, experiences, and interests in common. Ask yourself, "Is my audience made up entirely of rural people, townsfolk, or city dwellers?" A few years ago in New York City, I heard a speaker trying to make a generalization clear to his listeners. None of his listeners had lived outside metropolitan New York. He used one rural illustration after another. The audience was not impressed; nor were they enlightened by stories completely unrelated to their own experience. On the other hand, I heard a minister from North Carolina addressing a congregation of New Yorkers who drew all his examples and illustrations from New York City life. I was amazed at his familiarity with the problems his listeners faced, and they responded to his utilization of what was common and familiar to them.

Region. Mores and folkways vary from region to region; each area of the country has an inheritance and a flavor all its own. A wise speaker will adapt to these distinctive characteristics if his audience is composed of people from a single section. Biblical allusions are not likely to be lost on Southerners, and appeals to the pioneer spirit would be most welcome in the West, for example. Sectionalism and provincialism are, hopefully, dying, but regional differences remain, and you should adjust to them.

Nation. It may be relevant to your purpose if all the members of your audience are of the same nationality. They will then share the same cultural and linguistic heritage; they will likely observe the same customs and respect the same traditions. Adaptation to their national loyalty, appeals to their national interest, and allusions to their cultural inheritance may strengthen your speech.

Vocation. Members of the same profession or occupation have much in common in addition to their work: preparation, objectives, interests, concerns. They also usually share technical language peculiar to their vocation. When speaking to such an audience, you may assume their command of a common vocabulary. You need hardly define "due process" or "probable cause" for a group of lawyers; you could discuss speech therapy for the laryngectomized with a group of physicians without defining the term; and an audience of carpenters would not be confused by an unexplained reference to a "beveled edge." Common sense would dictate that you adapt your topic, your vocabulary, and your supporting materials to the vocation of such a homogeneous audience.

Socio-economic status. People who come from the same social or economic background have certain interests and objectives in common. If your audience is made up entirely or largely of persons from similar classes of society, you will have to take the fact into account in adapting your material. You might appeal to an audience of wealthy businessmen to follow a course of action because of humanitarian considerations, but you would hardly be able to move them by suggesting the action would raise their station in life.

Intelligence and education. Intelligence and formal education are not the same thing, but both are related to the ability of the audience to understand the speaker's vocabulary and follow his line of reasoning. You should, without condescension, try to adjust the language and the supporting details of the speech to the intelligence and training of your hearers. Intelligence will determine how quickly your listeners grasp an idea, and their educational background will indicate the amount and kind of information they have already been exposed to. If the audience is homogenous in these regards, take both factors into account.

Experience. It may be that your audience has shared some common experience or experiences that are relevant to your purpose. They may not only all be veterans, they may all be veterans of a particular military campaign; they may not only all be students, they may all have studied or flunked under the same teacher. If possible, analyze your audience in terms of common experiences.

Attitudes. Your audience may share a number of attitudes and opinions that bear directly on your topic and your purpose. Are they all cynics and hostile to religion? Then omit the quotations from Pope Paul and include others, drop the supporting opinion offered by the National Council of Churches and find another organization that takes the same point of view. Are they all conservative and suspicious of change? Then find evidence to show that your proposal is consistent with traditions long established and find supporting quotations from recognized conservative leaders. In short, find out if there is a climate of opinion in the group, and utilize it in your speech.

Interests. You may find that all the members of your audience have some particular interests in common. They may all be interested in foreign affairs, or sports cars, or philosophy, or abnormal psychology. If you discover in your analysis of the audience that they do share some enthusiasms, try to incorporate some references or illustrations that draw on this common affection.

Traditions and Practices. Your audience may share more than attitudes and interests; they may share customs—traditions and practices established long ago but respected and perpetuated. You might think that these customs ought to have been included simply as part of the discussion on common experience, but traditions are accorded a special reverence by most groups and they deserve special attention. You cannot insult or violate a group's customs with impunity; you must know them, understand them, and respect them.

Heterogeneity. Thus far in discussing audience analysis, we have thought in terms of similarities. In what ways are all the members of the audience alike, and how can a speaker adjust to those common factors? But it should be obvious that many audiences are in many ways not homogenous. What else must we take into account?

Well, we simply go through the list again—from Age to Traditions and Practices—and ask if the audience is diverse in each regard and, if so, what adjustment must we make to that fact. For example, if the ages of the listeners range from eight years to eighty, you should try to speak so as to be understood by the eight-year-olds without insulting the intelligence of the adults. If both sexes are present in the audience, I would not choose illustrations primarily from **Woman's Home Companion** or, for that matter, **Gent!** If your audience is made up of members of many different religions, I would be careful not to include quotations and illustrations from the experience of one religious group alone. If the listeners are from many different organizations and/or varied political persuasions, I would avoid citing only liberal Democrats as authorities or quoting exclusively from **The National Review** or **Ramparts.** If the hearers are from many different sections of the country, I would be careful not to refer only to one small part of the nation; if the listeners are from all over the world, I would try to avoid typical American provincialism; if the audience is made up of men from many professions, I would not narrow my supporting details to material from one vocation only.

Adapting to heterogeneity in the audience is a matter of common sense, but perhaps we all need to be reminded sometimes to use it.

The uses of public address

Every writer on public address since Aristotle has noted that speaking in public is a useful art as distinguished from a fine art. Men speak to accomplish some specific purpose or perform some function other than just to produce aesthetic pleasure. The fine arts may exist for their own sake alone, but men do not speak just to be talking. They expect their communication to accomplish some task and to elicit a specific response from the listeners.

Speaking, therefore, is a tool, an instrument, and it may be utilized in a number of different ways. Varied are the uses of rhetoric, which, like the knife, may be used either for healing or for harming, for surgery or for stabbing. It follows then that if you were to evaluate speaking, you would have to evaluate the end to which it is being used and the effectiveness with which it is applied.

Most rhetoricians, admittedly, have confined themselves to appraising speeches in terms of effectiveness. They have asked the question: Did the speaker accomplish what he set out to do? Did he utilize well the tool available to him, and was he successful in his operation? If his purpose was to inspire, were his hearers stirred? If his purpose was to persuade, were his listeners moved to agreement or action? In short, did he reach his goal?

Other questions, equally relevant but far more subjective and controversial, are less often asked. What was his purpose? Was the goal socially desirable? What were the consequences of his accomplishing (or failing to accomplish) his ends? Were the consequences socially desirable? These questions, you can see, are far more difficult to ask and to answer. It is much easier to discuss success (or failure) than values; it is much safer to discuss effectiveness than ethics. We shall turn to some of these difficult questions when we consider "Abuses of Public Address."

Although public address serves in many different ways, five pairs of uses might be listed.

Instructing and correcting

An important use of public address involves conveying information; speaking may be used to teach. To teach requires more than merely reciting data or rattling off facts. You must make the material coherent and clear; you must simplify and explain; you must organize and exemplify; you must define and interpret; you must hold attention and interest.

Public address is not only used to convey information to those who do not know; it is also used to correct misinformation of those who have been misinformed. Correcting erroneous "information" may be even more difficult than other forms of teaching. The error must be exposed tactfully before edification can take place.

Advocating and refuting

You may use public address to argue in favor of or against any idea or proposal. In a free society, decisions are made after deliberation. You may recommend a course of action and defend a proposition, or you may oppose a plan and disagree with a concept. The attempt to persuade an audience or dissuade it is an important use of public speaking. The cause you espouse, the alternative you suggest, or the belief you champion may depend upon your effective speaking for its acceptance. And the movement you fear, the proposal you resist, or the dogma you deplore may emerge victorious if you do not refute it with persuasive power.

Stirring and controlling

Speakers use public address to effect changes in the emotional states of groups. You may wish to arouse an audience; you will speak to stir its feelings and build its enthusiasm. Or you may, facing a group whose emotions are carrying it away, wish to pacify an audience; you will speak to calm it, to soothe its feelings, to subdue its irrational impulses, and to exert a disciplining, controlling, quieting influence. In either case, you will use speaking to affect the attitudes and emotions of your hearers.

Praising and blaming

Oral communication may be used to influence the listeners' impression of an attitude toward a person or persons. You may use the public platform to bestow praise on someone or to denounce him. Rhetoric is employed for communicating both commendation and censure, both praise and blame.

Accusing and defending

We also use speech for accusation and defense. The example that comes to mind immediately, of course, is that of the courtroom. There men speak, bringing charges against a defendant, challenging and attacking him; and the defendant and his lawyers speak, defending, excusing, explaining, denying, disproving, objecting, justifying, vindicating. Public address, then, may be used in the attempt to indict or convict on the one hand and to exonerate and clear on the other.

Summary

We have examined briefly five pairs of uses of public address: instructing and correcting—using speech for information; advocating and refuting—using speech for policy-formation; stirring and controlling —using speech for motivation; praising and blaming—using speech for evaluation; accusing and defending—using speech for justification.

Abuses of public address

You will remember that I said earlier, "if you were to evaluate speaking, you would have to evaluate the end to which it was being used and the effectiveness with which it was applied." If you were looking for abuses, then, you would examine the motives or goals of the speaker and the methods or means of the speaker. A speaker can misuse public address (it is an amoral tool of itself) either by seeking the wrong thing or by doing the wrong thing; "abuse" may lie in what he uses it for or in how he uses it.

You may be thinking to yourself: But isn't the author using moral or ethical terms and applying them to speech-making? Don't the very words "abuse" and "misuse" imply value-judgments? Isn't this kind of evaluation extremely subjective? Wouldn't the evaluation depend on your own value system? And I would have to answer to every one of these questions, "Yes." But, risky and relative as they are, I do not see how we can avoid asking them!

Judged in terms of effectiveness alone, Hitler was a good speaker. But I must deny that he was a **good** speaker; I personally can affirm only that he was an effective or a successful speaker. He **did** accomplish his goals; he **was** persuasive; his speech-making **was** a significant factor in his career. But I submit that, though he used the tool with cleverness and skill, he abused public address!

Surely, countless examples come to your own mind. Stalin, Mussolini, Fidel Castro, Sen. Joseph McCarthy—all would be recognized as effective speakers. All used platform oratory to instruct and correct, to advocate and refute, to stir and control, to praise and blame, to accuse and defend. But, because of motives or means or both, would you not hestitate to call all of them good speakers? Would you not agree that they misused the useful art of public speaking?

I believe that a man is responsible for his behavior and that he is as responsible for what he says as for anything else he does. Speech can exert awesome power; therefore, speaking entails awesome responsibilities. It seems to me that you and I can be held accountable for what we attempt to achieve through public address and for the methods of speaking we choose to accomplish our ends.

I do not apologize, therefore, for using words such as "abuse" and "misuse." They are the natural result of my conviction that we are accountable for what we say and the way we say it. But are there any guidelines to tell us what constitutes "abuse"? You must decide such issues for yourself, of course, but I have set up some tentative guidelines for my own thinking.

Ends

Judging a speech in terms of its ends is admittedly difficult, because the real objectives of the speaker may be different from the objectives he states and the results may be different from both. It would seem necessary, therefore, to examine all three aspects.

Stated objectives. Many speakers spell out their goals in their public utterances. Governor George Wallace made no secret of the fact that he was opposed to integration of the races; Adolph Hitler did not withhold his view of Germany's destiny to rule the world; Senator Joseph McCarthy made it clear he was determined to remove certain people from public service. Although there were doubtless other motivating factors in each of these instances, the speakers did give clear indications in their speeches of their intentions and goals.

Unstated objectives. Imputing motives to another person is a dangerous business, but we must recognize the fact that we cannot always take at face value the statements of a speaker with regard to his purposes. Unworthy causes are often—indeed, usually—defended and justified by rhetoric using the most worthy and noble terms. Jesus wryly observed that the Devil can quote scripture to serve his purpose. The point is that anyone can use lofty language and apply it to anything. Governor Wallace is not against equal rights; he is for **freedom!** Adolph Hitler was not for aggrandizement; he was for **justice** for Germany! Senator McCarthy was not for character assassination; he was **anti-Communist!** Of course!

Although we start analyzing ends with the speaker's stated objectives, we cannot stop there. We must examine other evidence—what else the speaker says, what the speaker does, and what the speaker is—and compare all the bits of evidence we can gather. We may find some evidence that is contrary to the stated objectives of the speaker and some that is downright contradictory.

No harm is done by speakers who are running as hard as they can for public office saying that they are not candidates. At times, it is necessary to play that noncandidate role. Timing of announcements is important in politics. But the noncandidates do not deceive anybody; more important, they do not intend to deceive anybody. But the point is clear: to analyze their real intentions you have to look beyond what they say.

And where do you look for other evidence? First, you look at the statement itself and ask yourself, "What does this really mean?" Writers on general semantics have pointed the direction here. They have reminded us to look beyond the words. The speaker who says, "My opponent is unfit for public office," may **mean** only "He and I are running for the same office and I want you to vote for me instead of him." The speaker who says, "This is not escalation; we are only expanding what we have been doing all the time," really means that he favors the act and he wants his listeners to use words with pleasant rather than unpleasant connotations in connection with it. A speaker may say, "Freedom is in danger in that neighboring land" when he means "We plan to invade" (or "intervene"), or he may say, "Aggression must be stopped" when he means "We intend to start bombing raids." If possible, get to the real meaning.

After you have studied the speech itself for hidden or covert meanings, look to other statements by the same speaker. To other audiences he may have expressed a different viewpoint. Did the speaker, for example, convey the same attitude when speaking before the D.A.R. or the American Legion he communicated to the League of Women Voters or Americans for Democratic Action? Compare what a man said in Shreveport with what he said in Chicago. Ask yourself if there were other public utterances that clarify or contradict the speech under study.

In addition to looking at the statement itself and at other statements on the same subject, you should examine deeds rather than words and consider whether they gibe. Words are strange things; they are not necessarily related to reality. A person can be saying "I believe in peace" while he bangs you on the head with a lead pipe. What a man says may not be borne out very well by his behavior. Only the most naive uncritically accept the words of any speaker—whether in private or from the platform. You must ask, it seems to me, whether statements of purpose are consistent with known facts of the speaker's behavior. You may get a clearer and more accurate picture of the speaker's motives and goals by observing what he does than by listening to what he says!

Actual results. A final question about ends should be considered: What were the actual results of the speech? What effects did the speech produce, and were those effects socially desirable? If a speaker says his purpose is to instill self-respect but his listeners consistently turn to violence, should you not raise some questions about the ends he serves? Though a speaker says he is serving the cause of God, if his listeners are encouraged to engender hate and animosity, can you not doubt the worth of his results? Are speakers not responsible, at least in some measure, for the effects their power of speech produces?

Summary. I simply cannot escape the conclusion that a person who speaks to advance unworthy causes or to accomplish socially undesirable goals and one whose speeches consistently produce socially undesirable results (such as chaos, anarchy, violence, or race hatred) is misusing public address. In fact, the better (more effective) a speaker he is, the graver the consequences and the more serious the abuse.

Means

Although the ways in which a speaker can misuse public address are almost countless, there are a number of practices we can point out as common and typical of methods that constitute abuse and ir-responsibility. This list is divided into two groups of practices—distractions and distortions.

Distractions are attempts to mislead; distortions are attempts to misrepresent. Distractions would divert the listener; distortions would deceive him. Both are methods that would lead audiences to conclusions apart from sound reasoning and complete, valid, accurate evidence.

Distractions. Distractions are efforts to divert attention from the issues. Techniques of evasion, they are attempts to sidetrack logical discussion and short-circuit rational processes. Distractions are deliberately introduced to mislead listeners. Their purpose is to confuse rather than clarify, to obscure rather than illumine. The following list gives only a few examples of such verbal smoke screens.

Attacking opponents instead of the arguments. If your purpose is to make a strong, logical case for your point of view, a personal attack leveled at a leading opponent of that point of view will not strengthen your case. Such an attack is obviously an attempt to confuse the audience and make them concentrate on **who** disagrees rather than on **what** the disagreement is. It is an attempt to substitute abuse for analysis. Some speakers in 1952 and 1956 attacked Adlai Stevenson for being divorced, and some attacked John F. Kennedy in 1960 for being Catholic. Admittedly, such tactics may succeed in confounding some listeners and in winning some votes, but the tactics were clearly those of evasion of issues.

If listeners should reach their decisions on the basis of sensible selection among alternatives, personal abuse is more than bad taste; it is subversion of rational discourse.

Emotionally charged language. Another tactic of distraction is the use of "loaded words," a favorite tool of demagogues. Verbal short-circuits of accurate reporting and sound reasoning, they are efforts to sway listeners with semantic sleight of hand rather than with evidence and logic. Words which, though full of sound and fury, signify nothing, should not be a part of the responsible speaker's vocabulary.

The speaker who solemnly told his audience that "the gooks and the hoods are invading the schools" really revealed nothing to discriminating listeners other than the fact that he did not like some of the students. The danger in "loaded words" is that they convey vivid (and often inaccurate) images and stir strong (though often irrational) passions. Do students invade schools? And what are **gooks** or **hoods** anyway?

Language of emotive appeal is one thing; language of anti-reason is another. Words which produce a reflexive rather than a reflective response and which will not stand reflective scrutiny are the language of distraction. Avoid them.

Appeals to baser emotions and prejudices. Appeals to hate, to hysterical fear, to racist bigotry, or to religious prejudices are also means of evading major issues. Emotional appeals are powerful instruments which the responsible speaker will use with great care and restraint.

The surgeon, to use the analogy again, knows the dangers as well as the benefits inherent in the use of his knife; he does not slash aimlessly. Even though he is cutting in a good cause, he does not cut at random. His good purpose will not justify poor technique! The speaker, too, must be careful about his techniques—even in support of a good cause. He must be especially careful about the use of emotional appeals.

Senator McCarthy's purpose, he said, was to save and preserve the security of the country. Surely no American would deny the worthiness of his goal; surely few would fail to doubt the worthiness of his methods. What is the appeal in the following sentence, and is it grounded in logic? "Today on July 9, 1952, the same men who delivered nearly half of the world to Communist Russia are still in control in Washington and in Moscow." Or this sentence: "Why, ladies and gentlemen, has this Administration deliberately built up Russia while tearing down the strength of America?" Or this: "Our job is to dislodge the traitors from every place where they have been sent to do their traitorous work." The appeals are to fear and hate, and to irrational fear and illogical hate, at that!

The coach who appeals to his team for their best effort and to his school for support because "Niggers are taking over sports and we gotta beat 'em" is appealing to the basest of motivations. He may stir his audience, but he does so at the expense of the audience's sound thinking and the society's stable functioning.

Red herrings. Red herrings are false issues raised to divert attention from the real issues. If a speaker must use such a method to distract his audience, he reveals the shakiness of his position on the major points of disagreement. How many times in discussions of public policy have we heard about "creeping socialism"? Trotting out such bogeys is inconsistent with serious, responsible public speaking.

Straw men. Anyone can construct an opposing argument and then tear it down. What talent does it take to attack a position no one would defend? What virtue is there in opposing a point of view no opponent would maintain? What value is there in creating a monster predestined for destruction? Such diversionary maneuvers may reveal the weakness of one's own position!

Distortions. Distractions are attempts by the speaker to get the listeners to focus their attention on something other than the point at issue; distortions, on the other hand, are attempts by the speaker to present the real issues inaccurately. The following incomplete list gives examples of all too common distortions.

Careless exaggeration. A few years ago I heard college debaters alleging that a few colleges in the East have a monopoly on all the scholarships in the country and that it is impossible for one in the "underprivileged South" to get a scholarship. Such sweeping generalizations exceed hyperbole; by verbal alchemy they turn half-truths into lies.

Broad generalizations are dangerous, and reasoning based on such generalizations can lead both speaker and audience astray. How would you classify such statements as: "The people of Appalachia are apathetic." "Socialism destroys liberty." "The American child has a simple concept of God." "The white Southerner is prejudiced." "Segregation is more rigid in the North than in the South." "Religious people are ignorant." I do not know how you react to them, but I feel very uncomfortable with all those generalizations. They are too all-inclusive to be accurate.

The speaker who uses sweeping statements may not intend to deceive his audience, but his faulty method misinforms his listeners and misinterprets facts. Since a speaker is responsible for what he says, the speaker must exercise care to be sure that what he says is accurate—completely accurate. Half-truths deceive as much, perhaps more, than outright lies. Careless exaggeration is distortion for which you will be held accountable when you speak.

Unwarranted conclusions. Reasoning lies in moving from a statement to a conclusion on the assumption that the logical leap is warranted. The first statement is a premise or a fact that prompts our leap to the conclusion; the conclusion is an inference we draw. Sometimes speakers draw inferences that are not justified. Although all members of an audience should be on guard against faulty reasoning, the speaker himself must bear the blame if he presents his listeners with unwarranted conclusions.

One speaker told his audience, "In 1954, only 4% of the students at this college were on scholarships of any kind. In 1956, 8% of the students were receiving financial aid. In 1960, the number of students receiving scholarships had risen to 12%. And today 20% of our students are receiving such assistance for their education. We can see that, thanks to the generosity of our college, all those who need financial assistance to pursue their college training may receive it." Is the conclusion warranted? The speaker claims to have proved that all who need aid now may receive it; in fact, he has only proved that the percentage of those receiving aid has increased. His figures have nothing whatever to do with the number of those in need and certainly do not prove that there is sufficient aid to supply all those who require it to go to that particular college.

Whether the speaker intended to deceive his audience or not, he did so if they accepted what he said. In any case, he misused public address by employing faulty logic.

Sophistry. Whereas careless exaggeration and unwarranted conclusions may or may not be deliberate on the part of a speaker, sophistry is a consciously chosen technique of distortion. Sophistry is specious but fallacious reasoning; it sounds good, it appears sound, but it is logically faulty. Based on intentionally deceptive arguments, sophistry requires cunning, craftiness, and trickery. The "trick" in sophistry lies in outwitting the audience, in putting something over on them, in convincing them with clever, but faulty, reasoning.

How would you analyze this line of reasoning? "The Free World is fighting the Communist World, which is the very essence of tyranny. Taiwan is in the Free World, fighting with us against Communism. The heroic government of Taiwan is dedicated to freedom, and we must fight to preserve it." Can you spot the use of one word to mean two quite different things? Can you identify the fallacy in the reasoning? Could you catch the trick if the line of argument had not been reduced to bare essentials?

All Sophistry is cleverly constructed, and it takes a very intelligent, informed, and critical listener to detect it. The audience hears the line of argument only once, after all. You cannot go back, reread it, and analyze it slowly and carefully. You must catch the flaw at the moment of utterance. That is why you must be on guard.

Sophistry, whether employed in college debating as the "Trick Case" or used on the public platform as a method of deception, is misrepresentation. And its use constitutes abuse of public address.

Distortion of facts. Figures, I am told, do not lie, but "statistics grew up and learned how." Some speakers have learned how, too. Accuracy is the standard of responsible public address; inaccuracy is a method of misuse. No speaker, no matter how noble his aims or how worthy his cause, has the right to misrepresent facts.

To say a survey was taken in 1963 when in fact it was taken in 1943, to say that there were one thousand cases when in fact there were one hundred, to say that a rug cost $24,000 when the receipts prove it cost $2,400 is to lie. And the speaker who presents false "information" to an audience is abusing the art of public address.

Withholding of evidence. You can deceive an audience as much by telling them only part of the truth or by giving them only some of the facts as by telling them outright falsehoods. If you know relevant information which would affect the opinion of the audience if they knew it too, and you withhold that information from them, you are practicing deliberate deception.

I remember a debater who a few years ago, to defend his loan case, introduced evidence in rebuttal which indicated that only two states had such loan programs. After the debate, he conceded that he had deliberately chosen an old quotation (whose date he did not give in the debate) and that in actual fact, at the time he spoke, far more states had such programs in operation. He felt absolutely no guilt about this withholding of information; he thought it merely clever strategy.

Withholding information from your audience, like any other method of deception, may temporarily advance your purpose, but it advances your cause by unworthy means. If it serves your cause, it does not serve it **well** and in the long run may not serve it at all.

William Trufant Foster, in his old book **Argumentation and Debating**, quoted William Herndon, Lincoln's law partner, who related many incidents that illustrated Lincoln's conviction that honesty must take precedence over all other considerations.

> In one case at law Herndon introduced a sham plea so devised as to deceive the opposing counsel and attain the desired end. When Lincoln saw the subterfuge, he asked, "Is this seventh plea a good one?" Herndon replied that it was. "But," asked Lincoln, "is it founded on fact?" On receiving a negative answer, Lincoln said: "Hadn't we better withdraw that plea? You know it's a sham, and a sham is very often but another name for a lie. Don't let it go on record. The cursed thing may come staring us in the face long after this suit has been forgotten."[1]

The audience, like the court, is entitled to "the truth, the **whole** truth, and nothing but the truth."

Misinterpretation of authorities. Almost every speaker, at some time

[1] William Trufant Foster, **Argumentation and Debating** (New York: Houghton-Mifflin Company, 1908), p. 315

or another, cites authorities and uses quotations. You may distort an author's point of view by deliberately misquoting him, choosing an accurate quotation that gives an incomplete and inaccurate picture of his stand, or by misinterpreting the statements attributed to him. The first method involves changing his words; the second involves pulling a quotation out of context; the third involves explaining an author's words in terms he would not grant.

To use the name, reputation, or words of another person in support of your assertions or contentions obligates you to represent the viewpoint of the authority accurately and fully. Not to do so is to abuse public address.

Misrepresentation of opponents' positions. In one of their public debates, Senator John Kennedy said that he never recognized his position when Mr. Richard Nixon stated it. I am not certain that he was accusing Mr. Nixon of distortion of his point of view, but if he was, the accusation is a serious one. An important part of persuasion is refutation of opposing arguments and answering objections of those who disagree with your stand. You have an obligation, however, to represent the opposition fairly. Any fool could attribute some illogical position to an opponent and then demolish it, but that is not fair to your opponents or to your audience. Those who disagree with your position have a right to have their views honestly reported, and your listeners have a right to know the real alternatives.

Summary. A speaker is responsible for what he says and the way he says it. Devious and dishonest techniques are as irresponsible and unworthy as socially undesirable goals, motives, or results. Distractions, which divert the listeners' attention from the real issues, and distortions, which attempt to deceive the listeners, are basically dishonest methods. And no cause or goal justifies using these means; instead, employing these devices constitutes misuse of the medium of public address.

Deliberative occasions: influencing

The campaign speech

Purpose

The word campaign was originally a military term denoting a series of military operations with a particular objective, but the term now has much broader meaning. A campaign is a series of organized, planned actions to accomplish a particular purpose. Ordinarily, campaigns are conducted by organized groups with specific goals in view.

When the word "campaign" is used today, most Americans think first, I suppose, of political campaigns: the organized efforts of political parties to elect their own candidates to public office. But there are many kinds of campaigns, and political campaigns are only one type. Ford and General Motors conduct sales campaigns; the YMCA and the Pep Club conduct membership campaigns; the Community Chest and your local church conduct financial campaigns; factories conduct production campaigns, to name only a few examples.

Campaigns, then, differ in terms of specific goals and sponsoring organizations, but they all have one thing in common: they are organized efforts to persuade. Campaigns are attempts by groups to influence people to believe or act in accordance with the group's purpose.

A campaign speech is a part of a larger effort, a larger movement, and it must be viewed in the context of the group drive. Its purpose is to advance the cause for which the group is working, to influence as many people as possible in behalf of the campaign's goals.

The general purpose of the campaign speech is to persuade listeners; the response desired is either agreement or action; the speaker tries to affect either the beliefs or behavior of his auditors. The word "persuasion" comes from two Latin words meaning "through sweetness"; the Romans may have heard my mother say, "You get more flies with sugar than with salt." In any case, the word has built into it the idea that men and women are influenced by attempts to appeal to them and that persuasion is an effort to attract supporters. The campaign speech is a persuasive speech that is part of a larger organized persuasive drive.

No matter what kind of campaign you are talking about, or taking part in, your speech must appeal to three groups of people: the committed, the uncommitted, and the opposed. Your purpose is to speak so that you will keep the allegiance of those already in sympathy with the campaign, win the support of those whose minds are open to the objectives of the campaign, and at least modify the attitudes of those in an opposing camp.

You should beware of the temptation to speak only to the partisans, and you should also beware of the temptation to neglect them. If you concentrate too heavily on those already in agreement with the aims of your drive, appealing to their partisan loyalties and overstating the case to capitalize on their enthusiasm, you may alienate some of the neutrals and independents and almost certainly you will add to the hostility of opponents. On the other hand, you should not take the committed for granted, because they must be encouraged to turn their agreement with your purposes into active support, and they may be able to influence their friends to join them in your cause.

Neutrals are the "swing" group in any campaign. Their support more often than not spells success or failure for the campaign. These people are uncommitted because they are unaware of the drive, uninformed about its objectives, indifferent to its efforts, hesitant to take a stand, deliberative in their judgments. In any case, their minds are still open on the subject and they can be influenced. There is a real opportunity to advance your cause by winning them.

Opponents sometimes change their minds, and you should not write them off as a lost cause. Given the right appeals and confronted with a logical case, some will modify and change conclusions they reached earlier. The 1948 presidential campaign is an excellent example of the fact that voters do change their minds, and campaigns can make a difference.

When you get up to give a campaign speech, remember that your goal is to hold the loyal, win the undecided, and soften opponents. To do so will require all of your persuasive skill.

Occasions

Campaign speeches are given on every conceivable kind of occasion. Dinners, picnics, rallies, conventions, club meetings, and any other form of gathering of people may be the setting for a speech during a campaign. The place may be a factory or an office, an auditorium or a field. But the time and place are of less importance in the campaign speech than the purpose. When and where are less vital than why the groups gather. Your opportunity to persuade may be enhanced by the occasion, but it will not be governed by the occasion.

Preparation

The campaign speech must be carefully prepared. A campaign is no hit-and-miss affair; the aim of the group is to succeed. And the speech that is an integral part of that series of activities must be planned carefully so as to contribute to achieving the goal.

Topics. Your subject will probably be dictated by the nature of the campaign. You would hardly push buying bonds if the campaign were designed to elect Joe Schmoe to Congress; you would not advocate repeal of the income tax as part of a campaign to raise money for the YWCA. "That," as the song says, "comes naturally." Your general subject area will be determined by the campaign itself.

Your specific topic, however, you must formulate yourself. If the campaign is to encourage people to buy defense bonds, you will probably not choose the simple topic "buy bonds." You will have to "get an angle"; you will have to decide what approach to the general subject area you will choose. Your theme might be: "Our servicemen are doing their part. Do yours." Or it might be: "Protect America and yourself; buy bonds."

In choosing the specific topic, consider what would appeal most to that particular audience on that particular occasion. What would be the most moving appeal that could be made on behalf of the campaign's objective?

When Senator John F. Kennedy spoke to the group of Houston ministers, he chose that aspect of the campaign most central to their interest: separation of church and state. The purpose of the campaign was to win the election, and every speech he gave in that campaign was an appeal for support and votes, but the specific approach to the appeal was on the basis of the fears, desires, and interests of the audience. That, unfortunately, does not come naturally; you will have to analyze the audience and select your best approach to the topic.

Materials. There are two major sources for the materials of your campaign speech: the issues of the campaign and the audience's attitude and aspirations. The issues dictate the logical points to be confronted, and the audience's attitudes and aspirations dictate the appeals to be made.

Issues are the question inherent in the proposal supported. They are the questions that must be faced and answered if an audience is to be convinced. They are the points of contention on which there is major disagreement (or clash).

There is little value in dwelling on those points on which everyone is agreed; you must come to grips with those matters which are the basis of opposition and doubt. You must face the issues and answer them! Issues, as I have said, are the basic questions. Your stand on these questions will be a major source of material.

Let us suppose that your favorite organization has launched a fund drive and you are going to be asked to speak to several groups in an effort to help raise the money. What are the basic issues of the campaign? What are the questions you must answer to get people to give? You might decide on a different set of basic questions, but it seems to me there are at least three: Is the money needed? Is the cause worthwhile? Who should bear the responsibilities of financial support of this cause? Once you clearly understand the issues involved, you can readily see the kind of material you must collect. In this case, you would need data on the financial situation of the organization so you could substantiate the necessity for additional funds; you would need material to justify the use of funds, showing the money would be spent on noble and worthy purposes; you would need material to establish the personal stake of listeners in the project, demonstrating that they are in some way involved in the project. The point is this: the issues dictate the content of your campaign speech, and where you go for the specific materials will depend on what the issues are.

In a fund-raising campaign, the topic question covering the entire drive would be "Why should people give?" In a political campaign, the fundamental question underlying the entire campaign would be either "Why should people vote for this particular party?" or "Why should people vote for this particular candidate?" In the case of the political campaign, there are personal issues as well as substantive ones. That is, there are questions about the candidates themselves in addition to questions about policy differences.

In a political campaign, you will have to face questions (issues) about the candidate's character and competence. In the presidential campaign of 1960, the character of "tricky Dicky Nixon" was an issue that Republicans had to face, and the religion of John Kennedy was an issue Democrats had to face. Now you might say that personal matters should not be issues in political campaigns, but let us be realistic. The masses do vote as much (or more) on their view of the person as they do on substantive issues. No campaigner can ignore the fact that the candidate **himself** must be sold—not just the candidate's ideas or programs. In fact, the campaigner must understand that the candidate himself is an issue in the campaign, and a major issue at that! And as I said earlier, the issues determine what material you seek and include.

Another source of materials is the audience to be persuaded. Of course, you must meet their logical objections (issues), but you must also appeal for their support in terms of their attitudes and aspirations. The two basic questions here are: What do these listeners already believe and what do they want (or hope or dream)?

In this case, your task is to identify whatever you are campaigning for with what the listeners already believe in, approve of, hope for. Do they believe in applying the Golden Rule? Show that your movement is a practical application of that principle. Do they believe in "An eye for an eye"? Then show that your cause is dedicated to justice. Are they interested in a better educational system for their children? Show that this program you advocate will benefit the schools. Are they preoccupied with thrift and saving? Then show that this program (even if it involves giving money) will save them money in the long run. The principle is simple: You must gain their support on the basis of what they **already** believe in and what they **already** want; listeners will not be won by any campaign in any other way.

Organization. Since the campaign speech is one designed to win adherents, you will doubtless want to use a psychological plan or arrangement rather than a purely logical one. There are a number of such plans from which you may choose. I would suggest that you select from these possibilities: Problem–Solution, Motivated Sequence, Refutation, Progression, Implication, and Reversal. All six have one point in common: the material is arranged in order to gain a maximum amount of appeal and to induce a minimum amount of negative responses.

Problem–Solution. After presenting some attention-getting material and before presenting the final appeal for action, you would have two major divisions of the speech: the presentation of a problem that needs to be solved and the advocacy of a specific solution to alleviate the problem.

The problem–solution plan gives the impression of a logical approach, although the problem may be presented in very emotional terms and the solution must be advocated not only through sound argument but also through emotional appeals. But the approach of "Here's what is wrong and here is what must be done to set it right" certainly has the appearance and appeal of common sense.

This approach is especially effective if there is not major opposition to your campaign's purpose. If your audience is made up primarily of those friendly or apathetic, this plan might be best suited for your purpose. Most people are not opposed to the work of the Red Cross or the Salvation Army, and if presented with a graphic need for funds to carry on their work, most people would respond favorably. Your task, then, would be to make vividly clear the work of the organization and its need for additional funds and then appeal for the listeners to do their part in meeting that need.

You should be reminded, however, that you should be certain your problem and solution match up; your "solution" should actually solve the problem you have described. Not long ago I heard a speaker paint a grim picture of accidents and deaths on the highways after which he advocated lowering the speed limits. He failed to demonstrate, however, that speed was the primary contributing factor to the accidents and deaths and that lowering the speed limits would appreciably lower the accident rate. In fact, he totally ignored evidence to the contrary. It is not enough to present a problem and a solution. You must relate the two and demonstrate that whatever you are campaigning for will actually solve (or at least appreciably affect) the problem you wish to attack.

Motivated sequence. Alan Monroe has popularized a variation of the problem–solution arrangement which he calls the Motivated Sequence. He divides the speech into five steps: the attention step, the need step, the satisfaction step, the visualization step, and the action step. The attention step, of course, is the introductory material designed to capture the interest of the audience and focus it on the subject at hand. The need step is the problem step in which the listeners are made aware of their own need for something or they are made aware that something needs to be done. The satisfaction step is that portion of the speech in which the solution is presented, in which the audience is told what will satisfy the need they have been made to feel or what specifically should be done to alleviate the problem. The visualization step is that portion of the speech in which the solution is graphically and imaginatively illustrated. It is that section of the speech in which the solution is "brought home" to the listeners so they can visualize themselves involved in the program. The action step, of course, is the closing punch, the final appeal for approval; it is the call for commitment.

The motivated sequence is an effective arrangement for all three groups of listeners. Much advertising, as Monroe rightly observes, is structured along these lines. The greatest virtue of this plan is that it works! Listeners will stay with you through this sequence, and the speech will build to a moving climax if properly handled.

Refutation. One possibility for arranging material, especially if there is strong opposition to your campaign, is that of refutation. After your attention-getting and orienting material in your introduction, and before your final appeal for agreement to your proposal, you would discuss a number of the major objections to your proposal and answer them.

If you are going to use the refutation approach, you must be careful to represent the point of view of opponents accurately, honestly, and completely, and you must be certain that your answers are powerful and persuasive. Misused, the refutation plan could easily become a straw-man tactic; properly used, it is a powerful instrument for allaying fears and calming doubts.

Obviously, you cannot answer all the possible arguments against your proposal or your candidate. But you can pick out the two or three major objections and deal with them. Take them one at a time and answer them one at a time. Marshal all the evidence and appeals you can to dispel that objection, summarize, and then move with a transition on to the next objection. Be careful that you do not give the impression you are attacking **opponents** or are belittling the opposition. Instead, maintain your goodwill throughout and make it clear that you are trying to clear up some misunderstandings. Take the point of view that you are answering serious questions and honest reservations, not that you are ridiculing the views or impugning the motives of those who hold them.

Progression. The plan of progression is sometimes called the "yes-response technique." In this arrangement of material, you move from the least objectionable idea to the most objectionable idea, trying all the way to lead your listeners without incurring their antagonism or resistance. It is best suited to indifferent or hostile audiences.

If you are facing an audience opposed to the purpose of your campaign, it would be foolish to begin by announcing your central theme at the outset. That move would only alienate them further. Why get up at the Young Democrats Club and open a speech with a call to support the Republican candidate for mayor? If that is your purpose, you must lead them there by a more subtle route.

Start with the ideas on which you and the audience could agree—there must be **something** on which you could agree—perhaps it is the need for honest officials in the town. Move from that point to another on which you and the audience agree. The idea is to move slowly toward more controversial points, on the assumption that if they get into the habit of agreeing with your points at the outset they will not resist much as you move further and further from their original position.

Implication. This arrangement of your material is called implication, because you seem to imply that there is only one sensible alternative to be followed—whatever, of course, you are campaigning for. The plan is sometimes called the "this or nothing technique." I have sometimes called it the "paint them into a corner plan."

Like the plan of progression, this plan is designed to affect neutrals and opponents without arousing undue hostility, and like the problem-solution approach, it gives the impression of being based on common sense.

Basically, the plan begins by facing a problem and then surveying the alternatives open for its solution. By raising and eliminating all the solutions but the one advocated, the speaker gives the inevitable impression that his proposal is the inescapably logical one.

Roosevelt's "Arsenal of Democracy" speech, delivered over the radio on December 29, 1940, offers an excellent example of the implication structure. He began by referring to the threat of the aggressive Axis powers and then dealt with the three alternatives for facing the threat. He mentioned neutrality as one possibility, and then demolished that alternative. Next he turned to appeasement as another possibility, and again he destroyed that alternative. Finally, he moved to the proposal he advocated, implying that it was the only sensible course open to the American people. He closed with a personal and emotional appeal to the American people to support that position.

The most important distinctive of the plan of implication is that you must lead the listeners to a compelling conclusion, eliminating other courses of action and leaving them with only your own from which to select.

Reversal. The last arrangement I am going to suggest you might use for the campaign speech is one that is especially designed for hostile audiences. It gives special attention to disarming the opposition before presenting the position of the campaigner.

In addition to the usual introduction and conclusion, the speech consists of two parts: material contrary (but not necessarily contradictory) to the point of view he will support and then material supporting the purpose of the campaign. By first mentioning factors that might lead listeners to take a position against the campaign, the speaker gives the impression of fair play and objectivity. He makes no pretense that all the weight of evidence is on one side and that there are no reasonable objections to the campaign. He concedes those points and discusses them openly. But he does not stop there! By means of a transition, he goes on to the other side of the picture and shows next that the preponderance of evidence lies on the other side with the campaign. He demonstrates that though there are some valid objections and reservations, the overwhelming amount of reasons and arguments lie on his side of the question.

Let us say that you are a part of a campaign to get voters to approve a new constitution for your state. The audience before whom you speak is rather conservative and suspicious of change. Reversal might be a good way of organizing your speech. You could begin by reminding your listeners that they must decide in the next election between the old constitution under which they are now being governed and the new one which has been proposed for their adoption. Then in the body you might spend time praising the old constitution and saying that for ninety years it had served the state well, and you might also spend some time conceding that the new proposed constitution is not a perfect document. You might even concede some of the most notable flaws in it. But you should remind the listeners that the flaws can be changed by amendments and that they are comparatively few. Then you could move to the advantages of the new constitution and show it superior, vastly superior to the old document.

This approach is the one that former Governor Bert Combs consistently used in advocating adoption of the revised constitution in Kentucky in 1966. By starting out, not with a direct attack on the old document, but with mild praise for it and with minor reservations about the new one, he made a favorable impression of candor and forthrightness. His opening concessions really strengthened his position when he came to that portion of the speech advocating change.

The only major danger in using this plan for a speech is that you may get the proportion out of whack, and the first section may outweigh the second. Be certain that you do not concede too much, undercutting your own case or your own candidate.

Applied to a political campaign, the technique of reversal is often quite effective. You can begin the body of the speech with praise for the opponent rather than an attack on him, and then move to the reasons why you must vote against that good man and support your own candidate.

Adaptation, style, and other distinctives

One factor you must remember when preparing the campaign speech is that men will support the campaign, not because you are enthusiastic and want them to, but because they have been led to want to do so. You must choose your language, then, not just to demonstrate your own feelings on the subject, but to generate feelings in your listeners.

Try to put yourself in the position of the listeners—adherents, neutrals, and opponents—and get their viewpoints first. Ask yourself: What would it take to convince me if I were indifferent or opposed? What would move me to vote, or buy, or give, or join? Then speak in those terms.

Here are a few simple, general suggestions: Speak in familiar words. Audiences will not be convinced by high-falutin language; they will be convinced, if at all, by words they understand. Speak in concrete words. You are campaigning for a specific goal, and you should speak in specific terms. Avoid abstract and general language. Speak in vivid, colorful words. Use emotive language; select words that stir up images in the minds of the hearers. Conjure up vivid impressions by choosing words with connotations you want to suggest. Speak in arresting phrases and striking sentences. Slogans are not an evil device, and they are often effective in a campaign. If possible, select phrases and sentences that will impress the listeners and lodge in their minds long after the speech is over. In brief, if you want the campaign to succeed, speak the language of the heart; you must move your hearers, to win them.

Presentation

Your delivery of the campaign speech must have the attributes characteristic of all effective platform speaking. But one extra word may be necessary: The speaker in a campaign must give some special attention to his **ethos,** his personal appeal, his (the word disgusts me but it is in common use) image! He must, above all else, appear direct, natural, and SINCERE. Unless you convey to your listeners that you really believe in what you are saying, unless you communicate your own sense of involvement and your own feeling of urgency, unless you transmit your personal conviction and commitment, you cannot hope to achieve your objectives for the campaign.

Specimen speech

On October 27, 1964, toward the end of the long campaign for the presidency, the Citizens for Goldwater Committee presented a nationwide television program in behalf of the candidacy of Senator Barry Goldwater of Arizona. The speaker was not a professional politician, but the well-known actor Ronald Reagan.

Mr. Reagan, a former liberal Democrat and then a conservative Republican, had been active for several years in the Republican Party in California. An experienced speaker, he had appeared on lecture platforms often. And he was no newcomer to television; he had been both an actor and emcee on nationally televised programs. This television program, however, was different from those on which he had appeared earlier. He was not playing a role or representing a product or firm; he was speaking for himself, his candidate, and his party.

The speech itself had been delivered first on June 25, 1964, and was repeated before a number of audiences during the course of the campaign. The address required only minor editing to adapt it to television.

The National Broadcasting Company carried the half-hour program from 9:30 to 10:00 p.m. The format was simple: the program began with a brief announcement, "The following program is sponsored by the Citizens for Goldwater Committee," and an even more brief introduction of the speaker, "And, now, Mr. Ronald Reagan."

The address was video-taped before an audience and broadcast later. The speaker stood behind a lectern on a platform which had a front railing covered with red, white, and blue bunting. He spoke from notes.

Mr. Reagan made a favorable impression on many viewers—or, to use current jargon, he conveyed "a good image." Indeed, his own political fortunes may have been enhanced by that appearance. In his thesis, Craig R. Smith commented:

> After the national broadcast—it was rebroadcast seven days later—money and support swelled for Senator Goldwater. The speech made over $600,000 [in contributions], Reagan became a national figure of political import; he was soon approached on the question of candidacy in California's gubernatorial primary.*

The text of the speech, entitled "A Time for Choosing," has been provided by the Republican National Committee and is reprinted with the permission of Mr. Reagan.

Thank you very much. Thank you, and good evening. The sponsor has been identified, but unlike most television programs, the performer hasn't been

---

* Craig R. Smith, "A Rhetorical Analysis of the Campaign Speaking of Ronald Reagan" (unpublished master's thesis, Queens College, August 1967), 114.

provided with a script. As a matter of fact, I have been permitted to choose my own words and discuss my own ideas regarding the choice that we face in the next few weeks.

I have spent most of my life as a Democrat. I recently have seen fit to follow another course. I believe that the issues confronting us cross party lines. Now one side in this campaign has been telling us that the issues of this election are the maintenance of peace and prosperity. The line has been used, "We've never had it so good!" But I have an uncomfortable feeling that this prosperity isn't something upon which we can base our hopes for the future. No nation in history has ever survived a tax burden that reached a third of its national income. Today 37 cents of every dollar earned in this country is the tax collector's share, and yet our government continues to spend 17 million dollars a day more than the government takes in. We haven't balanced our budget 28 out of the last 34 years. We have raised our debt limit three times in the last 12 months, and now our national debt is 1½ times bigger than all the combined debts of all the nations of the world. We have 15 billion dollars in gold in our treasury—we don't own an ounce. Foreign dollars claims are 27.3 billion dollars, and we have just had announced that the dollar of 1939 will now purchase 45 cents in its total value. As for the peace that we would preserve, I wonder who among us would like to approach the wife or mother whose husband or son has died in Viet Nam and ask them if they think this is a peace that should be maintained indefinitely. Do they mean peace, or do they mean we just want to be left in peace? There can be no real peace while one American is dying some place in the world for the rest of us. We are at war with the most dangerous enemy that has ever faced mankind in his long climb from the swamp to the stars, and it has been said if we lose that war, and in so doing lose this way of freedom of ours, history will record with the greatest astonishment that those who had the most to lose did the least to prevent its happening.

Well, I think it's time to ask ourselves if we still know the freedoms intended for us by the Founding Fathers.

Not too long ago two friends of mine were talking to a Cuban refugee, a business man who had escaped from Castro, and in the midst of his story one of my friends turned to the other and said, "We don't know how lucky we are." And the Cuban stopped and said, "How lucky you are! I had some place to escape to." In that sentence he told us the entire story. If we lose freedom here, there is no place to escape to. This is the last stand on earth, and this idea that government is beholden to the people, that it has no other source of power except the sovereign people, is still the newest and most unique idea in all the long history of man's relation to man.

This is the issue of this election, whether we believe in our capacity for self-government or whether we abandon the American Revolution and confess that a little intellectual elite in a far-distant capital can plan our lives for us better than we can plan them ourselves.

You and I are told increasingly that we have to choose between a left or right, but I would like to suggest that there is no such thing as a left or right. There is only an up or down—up to man's age-old dream—the ultimate in individual freedom consistent with law and order—or down to the ant heap of totalitarianism, and, regardless of their sincerity, their humanitarian motives, those who would trade our freedom for security have embarked on this downward course. In this vote-harvesting time they use terms like "the great society," or, as we were told a short time ago by the President, we must accept a "greater government activity in the affairs of the people." But they have been a little more explicit in the past, and among themselves—and all of these things that I now will quote have appeared in print. These are not Republican accusations. For example, they have voices that say "the cold war will end through our acceptance of a not undemocratic socialism." Another voice says that the profit motive has become outmoded; it must be replaced by the incentives of the welfare state, or our traditional system of individual freedom is incapable of solving the complex problems of the 20th century. Senator Fullbright has said at Stanford University that the Constitution is outmoded. He referred to the President as our moral teacher, and our leader, and he said he is hobbled in his task by the restrictions in power imposed on him by this antiquated document. He must be freed so that he can do for us what he knows is best. And Senator Clark of Pennsylvania, another articulate spokesman, defines liberalism as "meeting the material needs of the masses through the full power of centralized government." Well, I for one resent it when a representative of the people refers to you and me—the free men and women of this country—as "the masses." This is a term we haven't applied to ourselves in America. But beyond that, "the full power of centralized government"—this was the very thing the Founding Fathers sought to minimize. They knew that governments don't control things. A government can't control the economy without controlling people. And they know when a government sets out to do that, it must use force and coercion to achieve its purpose. They also knew, those Founding Fathers, that outside of its legitimate functions, government does nothing as well or as economically as the private sector of the economy. Now, we have no better example of this than the government's involvement in the farm economy over the last 30 years. Since 1955 the cost of this program has nearly doubled. One-fourth of farming in America is responsible for 85 percent of the farm surplus, three-fourths of farming is out on the free market and has shown a 21 percent increase in the per capita consumption of all its produce. You see, that one-fourth of farming that's regulated and controlled by the federal government. In the last three years we have spent 43 dollars in the feed grain program for every dollar bushel of corn we don't grow. Senator Humphrey last week charged that Barry Goldwater as President would seek to eliminate farmers. He should do his homework a little better, because he will find out that we have had a decline of 5 million in the farm population under these government programs. He will also find that the Democratic Administration has sought to get from Congress an extension of the farm program to include that three-fourths that is now free. He will find that they have also asked for the right to imprison farmers who wouldn't keep books as prescribed by the federal government. The Secretary of Agriculture asked for the right to seize farms—to seize farms through condemnation and resell them to other individuals. And contained in that same program was a provision that would have allowed the federal government to remove 2 million farmers from the soil.

At the same time there has been an increase in the Department of Agriculture employees. There is now one for every 30 farms in the U. S. and still they can't tell us how 66 shiploads of grain headed for Austria disappeared without a trace, and Billy Sol Estes never left shore! Every responsible farmer and farm organization has repeatedly asked the government to free the farm economy, but who are farmers to know what is best for them? The wheat farmers voted against a wheat program. The government passed it anyway. Now the price of bread goes up; the price of wheat to the farmer goes down. Meanwhile, back in the city, under urban renewal, the assault on freedom carries on. Private property rights are so diluted that public interest is almost anything that a few government planners decide it should be. In a program that takes from the needy and gives to the greedy, we see such spectacles as in Cleveland, Ohio, a million and a half dollar building, completed only three years ago, must be destroyed to make way for what government officials call a "more compatible use of the land." The President tells us he is now going to start building public housing units in the thousands where heretofore we have only built them in the hundreds. But FHA and the Veterans Administration tell us that they have 120 thousand units they've taken back through mortgage foreclosures. For three decades we have sought to solve the problems of unemployment through government planning, and the more the plans fail, the more planners plan. The latest is the Area Redevelopment Agency. They have just declared Rice County, Kansas a depressed area. Rice County, Kansas, has two hundred oil wells, and the 14,000 people there have over thirty million dollars on deposit in personal savings in their banks. When the government tells you you are depressed, lie down and be depressed!

We have so many people who can't see a fat man standing beside a thin one without coming to the conclusion that the fat man got that way by taking advantage of the thin one! So they are going to solve all the problems of human misery through government and government planning. Well, now if the government planning and welfare had the answer, and they've had almost thirty years of it, shouldn't we expect the government to read the score to us once in a while?

Shouldn't they be telling us about the decline each year in the number of people needing help? . . . The reduction in the need for public housing? But the reverse is true. Each year the need grows greater, the problem grows greater. We were told four years ago that seventeen million people went to bed hungry each night. Well, that was probably true. They were all on a diet! But now we are told that 9.3 million families in this country are poverty stricken on the basis of earning less than $3,000 a year. Welfare spending is ten times greater than in the dark depths of the depression. We are spending 45 billion dollars on welfare. Now do a little arithmetic and you will find that if we divided 45 billion dollars up equally among those 9 million poor families, we would be able to give each family $4,600 a year, and this, added to their present income, should eliminate poverty!

Direct aid to the poor, however, is running only about $600 per family. It seems that someplace there must be some overhead. So now we declare "War on Poverty" or "You, Too, Can Be A Bobby Baker!"

Now do they honestly expect us to believe that if we add 100 billion dollars to the 45 billion we are spending . . . one more program to the 30 odd we have, (and remember, this new program doesn't replace any, it just duplicates existing programs). . . . Do they believe that poverty is suddenly going to disappear by magic? Well, in all fairness I should explain that there is one part of the new program that isn't duplicated. This is the youth feature. We are now going to solve the drop-out problem, juvenile delinquency, by reinstituting something like the old CCC camps, and we are going to put our young people in camps; but again we do some arithmetic, and we find that we are going to spend each year just on room and board for each young person that we help $4,700 a year! We can send them to Harvard for $2,700! Don't get me wrong. I'm not suggesting that Harvard is the answer to juvenile delinquency!

But seriously, what are we doing to those we seek to help? Not too long ago, a judge called me here in Los Angeles. He told me of a young woman who had come before him for a divorce.

She had six children, was pregnant with her seventh. Under his questioning, she revealed her husband was a laborer earning $250 a month. She wanted a divorce so that she could get an $80 raise. She is eligible for $330 a month in the aid to dependent children program. She got the idea from two women in her neighborhood who had already done that very thing. Yet any time you and I question the schemes of the do-gooders, we are denounced as being against their humanitarian goals. They say we are always "against" things, never "for" anything. Well, the trouble with our liberal friends is not that they are ignorant, but that they know so much that is not so! We are for a provision that destitution should not follow unemployment by reason of old-age, and to that end we have accepted Social Security as a step toward meeting the problem. But we are against those entrusted with this program when they practice deception regarding its fiscal shortcomings, when they charge that any criticism of the program means that we want to end payments to those people who depend on them for a livelihood. They have called it insurance to us in a hundred million pieces of literature. But then they appeared before the Supreme Court and they testified that it was a welfare program. They only use the term "insurance" to sell it to the people. And they said Social Security dues are a tax for the general use of the government, and the government has used that tax. There is no fund, because Robert Byers, the actuarial head, appeared before a congressional committee and admitted that Social Security as of this moment is 298 billion dollars in the hole! But he said there should be no cause for worry because as long as they have the power to tax, they could always take away from the people whatever they needed to bail them out of trouble! And they are doing just that.

A young man, 21 years of age, working at an average salary . . . his Social Security contribution would, in the open market, buy him an insurance policy that would guarantee $220 a month at age 65. The government promises $127! He could live it up until he is 31 and then take out a policy that would pay more than Social Security. Now are we so lacking in business sense that we can't put this program on a sound basis so that people who do require those payments will find that they can get them when they are due . . . that the cupboard isn't bare? Barry Goldwater thinks we can. At the same time, can't we introduce voluntary features that would permit a citizen to do better on his own, to be excused upon presentation of evidence that he had made provisions for the non-earning years?

Should we not allow a widow with children to work, and not lose the benefits supposedly paid for by her deceased husband? Shouldn't you and I be allowed to declare who our beneficiaries will be under these programs, which we cannot do? I think we are for telling our senior citizens that no one in this country should be denied medical care, because of a lack of funds. But I think we are against forcing all citizens, regardless of need, into a compulsory government program, especially when we have such examples, as announced last week, when France admitted that their Medicare program was now bankrupt. They've come to the end of the road.

In addition, was Barry Goldwater so irresponsible when he suggested that our government give up its program of deliberate planned inflation so that when you do get your Social Security pension, a dollar will buy a dollar's

worth, and not 45 cents worth? I think we are for the international organization, where the nations of the world can seek peace. But I think we are
against subordinating American interests to an organization that has become
so structurally unsound that today you can muster a two-thirds vote on the
floor of the General Assembly among nations that represent less than 10 percent of the world's population. I think we are against the hypocrisy of assail-
ing our allies because here and there they cling to a colony, while we engage
in a conspiracy of silence and never open our mouths about the millions of
people enslaved in Soviet colonies in the satellite nations.

I think we are for aiding our allies by sharing of our material blessings
with those nations which share in our fundamental beliefs, but we are
against doling out money to governments, creating bureaucracy, if not socialism, all over the world. We set out to help 19 countries. We are helping
107. We spent $146 billion. With that money, we bought a $2 million yacht
for Haile Selassie. We bought dress suits for Greek undertakers, extra wives
for Kenya government officials. We bought a thousand TV sets for a place
where they have no electricity. In the last six years, 52 nations have bought
$7 billion of our gold, and all 52 are receiving foreign aid from us. No govern-
ment ever voluntarily reduces itself in size. Government programs, once
launched, never disappear. Actually, a government bureau is the nearest
thing to eternal life we'll ever see on this earth!

Federal employees number 250 million. These proliferating bureaus with
their thousands of regulations have cost us many of our constitutional safe-
guards. How many of us realize that today federal agents can invade a man's
property without a warrant? They can impose a fine without a formal hearing, let alone a trial by jury, and they can seize and sell his property in auction to enforce the payment of that fine. In Chico County, Arkansas, James
Wier overplanted his rice allotment. The government obtained a $17,000 judg-
ment, and a U.S. marshal sold his 950-acre farm at auction. The government
said it was necessary as a warning to others to make the system work!

Last February 19 at the University of Minnesota, Norman Thomas, six times
candidate for President on the Socialist Party ticket, said "if Barry Goldwater became President, he would stop the advance of Socialism in the
United States." I think that's exactly what he will do!

As a former Democrat, I can tell you Norman Thomas isn't the only man
who has drawn this parallel to socialism with the present administration.
Back in 1936, Mr. Democrat, himself, Al Smith, the Great American, came
before the American people and charged that the leadership of his party
was taking the party of Jefferson, Jackson, and Cleveland, down the road
under the banners of Marx, Lenin and Stalin. And he walked away from his
party, and he never returned to the day he died, because to this day, the
leadership of that party has been taking that party, that honorable party,

down the road in the image of the Labor Socialist Party of England. Now it doesn't require expropriation or confiscation of private property or business to impose socialism upon a people. What does it mean, whether you hold the deed or the title to your business or property, if the government holds the power of life and death over that business or property? Such machinery already exists. The government can find some charge to bring against any concern it chooses to prosecute. Every businessman has his own tale of harrassment. Somewhere a perversion has taken place. Our natural, inalienable rights are now considered to be a dispensation from government, and freedom has never been so fragile, so close to slipping from our grasp as it is at this moment. Our Democratic opponents seem unwilling to debate these issues. They want to make you and I think that this is a contest between two men . . . that we are to choose just between two personalities. Well, what of this man they would destroy . . . and in destroying, they would destroy that which he represents, the ideas that you and I hold dear.

Is he the brash and shallow and trigger-happy man they say he is? Well, I have been privileged to know him "when." I knew him long before he ever dreamed of trying for high office, and I can tell you personally I have never known a man in my life I believe so incapable of doing a dishonest or dishonorable thing.

This is a man who in his own business, before he entered politics, instituted a profit-sharing plan, before unions had even thought of it. He put in health and medical insurance for all his employees. He took 50 percent of the profits before taxes and set up a retirement plan, a pension plan for all his employees. He sent monthly checks for life to an employee who was ill and couldn't work. He provides nursing care for the children of mothers who work in the stores. When Mexico was ravaged by the floods from the Rio Grande, he climbed in his airplane and flew medicine and supplies down there.

An ex-GI told me how he met him. It was the week before Christmas, during the Korean War, and he was at the Los Angeles airport trying to get a ride home to Arizona, and he said that there were a lot of service men there and no seats available on the planes. Then a voice came over the loudspeaker and said, "Any men in uniform wanting a ride to Arizona, go to runway such-and-such," and they went down there, and there was a fellow named Barry Goldwater sitting in his plane. Every day in the weeks before Christmas, all day long, he would load up the plane, fly to Arizona, fly them to their homes, then fly back over to get another load. During the hectic split-second timing of a campaign, this is a man who took time out to sit beside an old friend who was dying of cancer. His campaign managers were understandably impatient, but he said, "There aren't many left who care what happens to her. I'd like her to know that I care." This is a man who said to his 19-year-old son, "There is no foundation like the rock of honesty and fairness, and when you begin to build your life upon that rock, with the cement of the faith in God that you have, then you have a real start!" This is not a man who could carelessly send other people's sons to war. And that is the issue of this campaign that makes all of the other problems I have discussed academic, unless we realize that we are in a war that must be won. Those who would trade our freedom for the soup kitchen of the welfare state have told us that they have a utopian solution of peace without victory. They call their policy "accommodation." And they say if we only avoid any direct confrontation with the enemy, he will forget his evil ways and learn to love us. All who oppose them are indicted as warmongers. They say we offer simple answers to complex problems. Well, perhaps there is a simple answer . . . not an easy one . . . but a simple one. If you and I have the courage to tell our elected officials that we want our national policy based upon what we know in our hearts is morally right, we cannot buy our security, our freedom from the threat of the bomb by committing an immorality so great as saying to a billion human beings now in slavery behind the Iron Curtain, "Give up your dreams of freedom, because, to save our own skin, we are willing to make a deal with your slave-masters." Alexander Hamilton said, "A nation which can prefer disgrace to danger is prepared for a master, and deserves one!" Let's set the record straight. There is no argument over the choice between peace and war, but there is only one guaranteed way you can have peace . . . and you can have it in the next second . . . surrender! Admittedly there is a risk in any course we follow. Either course we follow other than this, but every lesson in history tells us that the greater risk lies in appeasement, and this is the spector our well-meaning liberal friends refuse to face . . . that their policy of accommodation is appeasement, and it gives no choice between peace and war, only between fight and surrender. If we continue to accommodate, continue to back and retreat, eventually we have to face the final demand—the ultimatum.

And what then, when Nikita Khrushchev has told his people he knows what our answer will be? He has told them that we are retreating under the pressure of the cold war and some day when the time comes to deliver the ultimatum, our surrender will be voluntary because by that time we will have been weakened from within spiritually, morally and economically. He believes this because from our side he has heard voices pleading for a peace at any price, pleading for "peace at any price," or "better Red than dead." Or as one commentator put it, he would rather "Live on his knees than die on his feet." And therein lies the road to war, because those voices don't speak for the rest of us. You and I know and do not believe that life is so dear and peace so sweet as to be purchased at the price of chains and slavery. If nothing in life is worth dying for, when did this begin. . . . Just in the face of this enemy . . . or should Moses have told the children of Israel to live in slavery under the Pharoahs? Should Christ have refused the cross? Should the patriots at Concord Bridge have thrown down their guns and refused to fire the shot heard 'round the world? The martyrs of history were not fools, and our honored dead who gave their lives to stop the advance of the Nazis didn't die in vain! Where, then, is the road to peace? Well, it's a simple answer after all. You and I have the courage to say to our enemies, "There is a price we will not pay." There is a point beyond which they must not advance! This is the meaning in the phrase of Barry Goldwater's "Peace Through Strength!" Winston Churchill said that destiny of man is not measured by material computation. When great forces are on the move in the world, we learn we are spirits, not animals. And he said there is something going on in time and space, and beyond time and space, which, whether we like it or not, spells duty. You and I have a rendezous with destiny. We will preserve for our children this, the last best hope of man on earth, or we will sentence them to take the last step into a thousand years of darkness.

We will keep in mind and remember that Barry Goldwater has faith in us. He has faith that you and I have the ability and the dignity and the right to make our own decisions and determine our own destiny.

Thank you.

Questions for specimen speech analysis

1. Did Mr. Reagan attempt to appeal to Democrats and independents as well as committed Republicans? Did he attempt to appeal to liberals as well as conservatives?

2. Was the purpose (enlisting support for Senator Goldwater) clear throughout the speech? Was there a clear central theme, such as "Vote for Senator Goldwater" or "Senator Goldwater is worthy of our support"?

3. Would the speech be likely to advance the Senator's candidacy? Would this speech help win votes?

4. What issues did Mr. Reagan discuss? Did he discuss the issues logically? Persuasively? What questions about the candidate did Mr. Reagan attempt to answer? Had you been a listener, would the answers have been satisfying and effective?

5. Did Mr. Reagan identify Senator Goldwater's candidacy with prevailing American attitudes and aspirations? If so, how?

6. Was Mr. Reagan's speech organized in any kind of identifiable pattern? Was the structure clear and easy to follow? Were the parts logically related? Did one idea flow smoothly into the next?

7. Was the introduction arresting? Did the conclusion have a persuasive punch?

8. Did Mr. Reagan support his generalizations with sound reasoning and valid evidence?

9. Was the language well-chosen? Did he use clichés, vague abstractions, or "loaded words"? Were all the sentences clear and well-constructed? How would you describe Mr. Reagan's style?

10. What adaptation did Mr. Reagan make to the medium of television?

11. How would you evaluate the speaker's attempts to enhance his own credibility?

The legislative speech

Purpose and occasion

If you are a member of a policy-making body which operates under the rules of parliamentary procedure, you will likely give a legislative speech. Legislative speeches are given not only in legislatures or parliaments or conventions; the term includes speeches delivered in all organized groups where courses of action are debated.

If the faculty of the Department of Speech meets, deliberates, and votes, staff members will give legislative speeches; if your fraternity holds business meetings, brothers will give legislative speeches; if the local chapter of the D.A.R. meets, the members will give legislative speeches. Such speeches, then, are given on a variety of occasions which have but two things in common: they are deliberative in nature and they function according to parliamentary procedure.

Generally, speeches are given in such assemblies either to propose, support, or oppose specific measures being considered for adoption by the group. The goal is rather immediate. Either you are trying to influence people to vote for the motion or to persuade them to vote against it. As in the case of the campaign speech, you must take into account those favorably disposed, those strongly opposed, and those still undecided. Obviously, you have the best chance of influencing those who have not yet made a decision on the proposition, but you should not rule out opponents until the votes are actually cast. Speechmaking can exert a persuasive influence!

If a motion has been brought up and seconded in a parliamentary body, the group is going to have to act on the measure in some way.

The audience, therefore, is a rather unique one; every member must eventually take a stand on the proposal. You should have their attention, because they are all involved in the decision-making process and they all have a responsibility with regard to the group's action.

If the members of the assembly—the Student Government, for example—are elected representatives of a larger population, they may be keenly aware of their responsibilities, since they are responsible not only to their consciences but to their constituents.

In any case, you are speaking to a select audience rather than to a general one. And this audience is not only more involved in the point at issue, but is probably also more informed than the general public on the matter being considered. Background material and simplification of the complexities, which would be necessary for the masses in a campaign speech, are unnecessary in the legislative speech.

This speech has a major purpose: to influence the outcome of the vote on the proposal. You hope to encourage the faithful supporters and entice enough of the uncommitted to insure the passage or defeat of the motion.

Your legislative speech may have another purpose as well. You may make a speech on a motion, even though you are quite certain that your point of view is going to be defeated when the votes are counted. You may be looking beyond the immediate vote. You may be preparing the way for a later encounter when today's minority will gain enough adherents to become the majority. Or you may be looking beyond the confines of the assembly hall to the larger audience, and speaking for a lost cause, to take your stand and let the public know your unequivocal position. Your purpose may be not to say, "Vote for (or against) this bill," but to say, "Here I stand."

In either case, your purpose is to influence men. But the audience at which you aim your influence may be either the immediate face-to-face audience which must vote at once on the measure, or the larger unseen audience which at some other time and place may decide the issues in a different way.

Preparation

Topics. Your topic will be dictated either by the motion already before the assembly on which you are asked to take a stand, or it will be determined by your convictions on what actions the group needs to take. If you perceive that there is something the group needs to do, then propose it and support it. If you believe that there is some stand the body ought to take, advocate it. If you are convinced the organization is about to make a mistake, call it to the membership's attention and oppose it.

Your topics, in short, will arise from the life of the group and from your awareness of the major issues confronting the assembly of which you are a part.

Materials. Out of what materials will you construct this speech? Three kinds of material should be woven into your address: sound reasoning, valid evidence, and worthy appeals.

Reasoning. In a legislative speech, you take a position on a controversial topic. You take a stand, which you must justify logically. Reasoning, then, is an integral part of the legislative speech. You must give the reasons for supporting or opposing the measure, and the reasons should be sound and directly related to the proposition being debated.

There is no need in this small book to go into detail on the various forms of reasoning. Briefly, we will consider four types of reasoning you might employ: induction, deduction, analogy, and sign.

Inductive reasoning is that form in which generalizations are drawn from specific instances. You move from the specific fact or example (hopefully, from a number of similar, related facts or examples) to a general conclusion. It is a means of drawing inferences regarding an entire class from observation of a selected portion of the class. We reason in this fashion all the time. It is not possible to observe all the examples in the world of everything about which we wish to speak, so we generalize, assuming that the examples we know are typical of the entire group.

One student in a speech opposing the formation of fraternities and sororities on our campus cited the example of the death of a student in a fraternity hazing incident at a western university several years ago. He made the inference that all fraternities were guilty of dangerous hazing practices and that they should be outlawed for that reason. The speaker cited only one example taken from the experience of one fraternity at one university, but he generalized about all fraternities on all campuses from the example. He not only did not establish that the practice he alleged was universal, he did not even establish that it was typical or widespread. His reasoning was faulty.

Be certain that you observe enough instances to be sure that the generalization really applies to the entire class of objects being described, and be certain that the examples you observe are a fair sample. Do not pick out a few exceptions and declare that they are typical.

Deductive reasoning is that form in which you move from a generally accepted premise to a specific conclusion. Ordinarily, many of the inferences are left unstated and must be supplied by the listeners.

The speaker who argues: "If elections are held now in Erehwon, the Communist ticket will surely be elected; we must prevent those elections from taking place," is reasoning deductively. That is, he is reasoning from a general premise to a particular conclusion. His assumption seems to be that we must prevent Communists from coming to power in any country in the world, no matter how democratic the means by which they achieve power and no matter how undemocratic the means by which we intervene. If he were to state the underlying assumption so starkly, he would have more trouble persuading listeners, but uncritical auditors might easily accept his argument without any examination of the logical underpinnings.

What assumptions are basic to the following line of reasoning? "A Communist Cuba is a military threat to the security of the United States. We should destroy the present government of Cuba by any means at our command." Does the speaker not assume that any Communist country is a **military** threat to the United States and that, since Cuba is now a Communist country, it must be a military threat? Is this reasoning sound? Is it founded on a logical premise? Do you grant the truth of the presumption that all Communist countries are military threats to the United States?

When a speaker moves from a generalization to a conclusion he should be as certain as he can that the move is warranted. Are the premises grounded in fact, and is the leap from premise to conclusion logically justified? Or, stated another way, are the statements on which the conclusion is based logically defensible, and if so, does the conclusion logically follow from those premises?

If you use deduction, and you will, test it carefully. Ask yourself what steps in the line of argument you are leaving out and expecting your listeners to supply. And ask yourself if you could defend—indeed, if you really believe—all the unstated assumptions which are necessary to your argument.

Analogies are commonly used as a means of persuasion. A form of comparison, an analogy is based on the assumption that what is true in one instance will be equally true in a similar instance. If you know what obtained in one case, you can make an inference that the same thing will obtain in a similar, but unknown case. If you compare two things of the same kind (for example, two states, two colleges, or two nations), the analogy is literal; if you compare two things of different kinds (a person and a tree, for example), the analogy is called figurative. Both, in my judgment, are forms of reasoning, though there are writers who think figurative analogies only stylistic devices. Speakers who use figurative analogies **think** they are reasoning and they certainly draw inferences from those analogies, so I believe we must analyze them as a form of reasoning, however shaky and suspect they may be!

An excellent example of a literal analogy was provided by a student at Eastern Kentucky University. He said: "Our sister institution has led the way. The University of Kentucky has adopted a new revised code for the regulation of student affairs, and our university should do the same. U.K. and Eastern are similar in many respects. We both serve the same state; we have similar student bodies; we are responsible to the same public officials; we are subject to the same pressures; we exist in the same social and cultural climate; and until recently we have had similar rules. Those rules have not worked well at either institution, and U.K. has had the wisdom to change them. We, too, should adopt a liberalized student code and start treating our students as adults!" To test his analogy, we would ask two questions: (1) Are the facts alleged true? and (2) Are the two institutions being compared similar in the essential and relevant respects?

A few years ago, Congressman Stratton of New York gave an excellent example of a figurative analogy, an exact copy of which is unavailable but which could be paraphrased as follows: "When a gunslinger shoots his way into the ranch house and holds the rancher's family captive, the sheriff and his posse have several alternative courses of action. They could either go in shooting, in which case they are certain to get the gunslinger, but they are also likely to hurt the family. Or they could surround the house and try to starve out the gunslinger, in the hope that he would give up before the family suffered too much. Or they could surround the house and harass him with tear gas, which would make life unpleasant for the family but not kill them and would surely rid them pretty soon of the troublesome gunslinger. Now Castro is like that gunslinger; he has gone in and captured Cuba and is holding those people hostage. And we have those alternatives. I am in favor of the isolation and harassing treatment." We must ask the same basic questions. Are the facts accurately presented in this picture of the Cuban Revolution? And are the comparisons justified, or are the things compared really similar in important respects? Specifically, is Castro similar to a Western gunslinger in that he came from outside, invaded a defenseless people, and is now holding them at gunpoint against their will? And if you grant that similarity—that Fidel Castro is an international outlaw—would you grant the second comparison which makes the United States the sheriff of the world or at least of the hemisphere? The posse is not clearly identified in the analogy, though it could be the Organization of American States. It certainly is not the United Nations! But do the similarities, on which the analogy must stand or fall, hold up?

When you employ an analogy, whether literal or figurative, test it for soundness. However colorful it may be, use it only if it meets the logical tests.

When you reason from "sign," you make an inference that the presence or absence of one factor indicates the presence or absence of another factor. The old saying, "Where there's smoke there's fire," is an excellent example of reasoning from sign. One thing is taken to be an indication of something else.

When we see the budding of the trees, we assume that spring is approaching; when we see leaves turning red and gold, we conclude that fall is arriving. But such inferences are simple ones. We use sign reasoning for much more complex leaps—and those more complex leaps are also much less certain. For example, Barry Goldwater insisted on many occasions that the Soviet Union was weak and would back down before any firm demonstration of force. He made this inference about weakness on the basis of sign reasoning. He believed that the removal of Soviet missiles from Cuba was a sign of weakness. Such signs are more difficult to interpret. Could not the removal of those missiles as easily be a sign of something else other than weakness, and could not a policy based on the assumption of weakness have disastrous effects if mistaken?

You will doubtless make interpretations of events and rely at times on sign reasoning, but you should be as certain as possible that the indicators lead almost conclusively to the inference. Signs can easily mislead you.

Evidence. Evidence is something that makes another thing evident or clear; it tends to establish a point or prove a contention; it forms the basis for believing a proposition. Evidence is the supporting material of the persuasive speech.

In your legislative speech, you not only will have to give logical reasons to support your point of view, you will also have to supply evidence to bolster it. Evidence consists of facts or opinions used to support an argument.

Facts are bits of data which can be verified. They are perceived by the senses, and any rational person observing them should perceive the same thing. It was a fact, for example, that Jack Ruby shot Lee Oswald. Many of us **saw** the act. It is not a fact, but a judgment, as to whether that act constituted murder. Any rational person observing could have seen Ruby shoot Oswald; the act could be verified by the senses. But we do not arrive at conclusions such as guilty or not guilty of murder by sense perception, but rather through value judgments. "There are one million American servicemen serving abroad" is a statement of fact (which may be either true or false), because its accuracy can be checked. "There are too many American servicemen in Europe" is not a statement of fact, but an opinion, because its accuracy cannot be checked in the same way.

You may use several kinds of factual information to support your contentions. You may use single facts. For example, you might support the contention that America should increase its financial aid to education with the statement, "Americans spent more on cigarettes last year than they spent on higher education." (Is that statement true? Is it a fact?) Or you might oppose the calling of a national constitutional convention by stating, "Since the Constitution was adopted, the United States has never called a constitutional convention!" (Is that statement accurate? Is it a **fact?** Remember that facts can be checked and that anyone checking should get the same answer.)

In addition to isolated facts, you might use statistics for support. Statistics are numerical facts which have been assembled, classified, and tabulated. Usually they are used to make generalizations about a rather large population on the basis of data compiled on a representative sample. Public opinion polls, for example, present statistics on the division of attitudes of a number of people interviewed. From such polls, the President makes inferences (and so do the rest of us) about what "Americans" are thinking.

You should be quite cautious in the use of statistics. Someone has said that figures do not lie, but statistics grew up and learned how. There is a delightful book entitled **How to Lie With Statistics.** Statistical data may be effectively employed if you interpret them clearly and accurately and apply them specifically to the point you are making.

Not only can statistics be misused, they can be dry! The recitation of numbers can be deadly dull. A statement such as, "Major crime was up 25 percent in our city last year" means little to most audiences. Statistics must be made to come to life; they must be made vivid and graphic if they are to render persuasive support to your proposal. Apply the statistics, if possible, to your listeners. If the statistics indicate that one out of ten Americans will undergo treatment for mental illness, and you are pleading for better facilities for the mentally ill, do not present the statistics with the statement, "ten percent of the American people will spend some time in a mental hospital." Why not say to the thirty people in the room, "If the group is typical here, three of the thirty of us will need hospitalization for mental illness at some time in our life." Bring the statistics as close to home as possible.

Avoid overuse of statistics. Use only as many as you need to support your case. Do not recite long lists of numbers. You will bore your listeners and defeat your purpose. Use statistics sparingly, and use them wisely.

Examples are specific instances and may provide valuable support for some point you are trying to make. They provide the specifics to establish the generalization. One speaker used a number of examples to strengthen his point: "Many colleges and universities are abolishing social fraternities and sororities. Williams has done so. Dartmouth has done so. . . ." (and he proceeded to list a number of schools to exemplify his contention). The example supplies particular cases; it gives concrete details.

In addition to factual evidence, you may also use opinions or testimony. Your listeners may not take your assertions on face value, but they may be quite willing to accept the opinions of certain authorities who are in agreement with your position. The testimony of an expert, giving his interpretation of facts or expressing his judgment on the point at issue, may be an invaluable aid in winning support for your position.

You must be certain, when choosing testimony to introduce into your speech, that the person is a competent authority on the subject and that the listeners know and respect his qualifications to express a judgment. Unless the "expert" is respected by your listeners and they account him credible, you might as well not quote him at all.

Organization. Like the campaign speech, the legislative speech is designed to win adherents, and you may want to choose for your material one of the psychological arrangements suggested in the section on the campaign speech.

You might, however, choose a much more direct approach; in the introduction you could announce the position you intend to defend and in the body give the reasons for that position on the question. The conclusion, then, could be a summary, a recapitulation, a quotation, or a closing appeal for concurrence. This direct approach is especially suited to the legislative speech because of the select nature of the audience to whom the appeal is directed.

Presentation

All of the usual requirements of effective public communication apply to the legislative speech. You should be direct, conversational, spontaneous, vital, varied, and free from distracting mannerisms. You should perhaps be warned against a faulty delivery adopted by some speakers in deliberative assemblies: shouting or declaiming the speeches. You should not **sound** like you are making a speech; you should sound like you are talking naturally and conversationally to your friends. Pushing the ideas at your listeners by increasing the volume or pitch of your voice does not enhance communication or insure acceptance. Do not get "oratorical"! Instead deliver the speech extemporaneously, earnestly, and enthusiastically.

Specimen speech

On March 14, 1967, Senator Mark Hatfield, the junior senator from Oregon, introduced a bill entitled "Armed Forces Improvements Act of 1967." This bill, Senate Bill 1275, provided for the early transition to a fully voluntary system of procuring military manpower. It proposed upgrading the economic and educational benefits of the members of the armed forces so as to attract a sufficient number of volunteer career personnel.

The bill was received, read twice by its title, and referred to the committee on Armed Services, where it died a quiet death. Senator Hatfield's speech in defense of his proposal, delivered for the record, in the Senate on March 14, 1967, follows. The text is taken from the **Congressional Record** and is printed with Senator Hatfield's permission.

Mr. President, the debate over our present system of military conscription has been continuing since the draft was initiated in 1940. It has had strong supporters, such as General Hershey who sees the draft as the only possible method of meeting military manpower needs and its vehement detractors, such as the late Senator Arthur Vandenberg who, in 1940 described it as "repugnant to the spirit of democracy and the soul of republican institutions."

Recently, the focus of the debate on the draft has shifted from an attack on, and defense of, this system to an argument concerning the best method of eliminating the many inadequacies in our current draft law. The pertinent question has become "What system of military manpower recruitment best meets today's realities and needs?" The answer to this question lies in the identification of a system that is based on the following criteria. This system must: First, preserve the maximum amount of individual liberty and freedom from unjustified intrusion by the government; second, be fair in its application so that every young man receives equal treatment and no young man is required to make sacrifices that are not demanded of his peers; and third, the system must provide for maximum national security and must economically provide the armed services with the needed quantity and quality of men.

It can very definitely be shown, I believe, that the current draft system does not adequately meet this criteria. I feel very strongly that each man has a moral obligation to serve his country, but he must be granted the freedom to accept his responsibility and the right to determine what form his service shall take. Any time a man is forced, against his wishes, into military service his individual liberty and freedom of choice have been denied. Daniel Webster spoke against a draft proposal in 1814:

> The question is nothing less than whether the most essential rights of personal liberty shall be surrendered, and despotism embraced in its worst form.

The surrender of this right to liberty can only be justified when there is no other alternative to conscription and when it is absolutely necessary for national survival. There have been periods in our history when, perhaps, conscription was the only alternative to destruction. But circumstances have changed and forcing men into service is no longer the only alternative in meeting military manpower needs.

The draft does not meet the second criterion of just and equal application to all young men. The inequities of the draft have been much discussed and well documented. Critics have pointed to the inequities of college deferments that discriminate in favor of the wealthier and brighter young men who can stay in school until they are 26. According to Thomas Morris, Assistant Secretary of Defense, of the men reaching age 26 as of June 1964, only 40 percent of the college graduates had served while 60 percent of the college dropouts, 57 percent of the high school graduates and 50 percent of the non-high-school graduates had been required to serve.

Also criticized have been deferments that excuse from draft liability those who can obtain an occupational or hardship deferment, those with criminal or unacceptable moral backgrounds, and those who marry young. And the nature of the Selective Service System, itself, has produced inequities. The 4,084 local draft boards have been granted great latitude in interpreting and administering draft regulations and this lack of clear and nationally uniform standards has led to situations where cases with similar circumstances have been handled entirely differently in various parts of the country.

But the most basic inequity of the current draft system, and an injustice that is often camouflaged by listings of specific inequitable policies, is the fact that a smaller and smaller minority of our young men is carrying the burden of national defense. The principle of universal sharing of the national defense responsibility, upon which the present system was sold to the public years ago, is a transparent falsehood today. Currently, only about 46 percent of the men reaching age 26 have seen military service. By 1974, at pre-Vietnam force levels, only 34 percent of those reaching age 26 will be required to serve. Even under current crisis conditions, the military drafts only about 300,000 men a year out of a draft-eligible manpower pool that totals nearly twelve and a half million.

This manpower surplus has spawned the many inequities of the current draft system by eliminating the feasibility of requiring all young men to share the burden of insuring national security. We cannot tolerate the injustice of a system that capriciously requisitions 2 years out of the lives of some young men while allowing others their liberty.

The third criterion that a military manpower recruitment system should meet is that of efficiently and economically providing the armed services with the needed quantity and quality of men. It must be conceded that the current system of conscription does provide the necessary quantity or numbers of men. But even this success of the draft system must be qualified by the great costs and inefficiencies that result from this method of meeting military needs. Draftees—who have been taken from civilian life against their wishes—spend their 2 years of military service counting the days until they get out. As soon as the required period is over, they inevitably return to civilian life. Their empty bunks are filled with more draftees and the cycle continues. This high turnover is extremely inefficient and uneconomical. According to the latest figures available from the Department of Defense, the current turnover rate among draftees is about 95 percent. Since the full cost of training of a foot soldier is a minimum of $6,000, the total training cost for the draftees now serving and who will leave the service at the end of their 2-year obligation is $3 billion.

The draft, then, provides the necessary quantity of men only at great cost. But even this huge expenditure cannot buy the quality of military personnel that is needed. Since the draft was instituted, the basic nature of military strategy and technology has changed. The Universal Military Training and Service Act was designed to supply the armed services with large numbers of men, but large numbers of men in uniform are no longer appropriate to the nature of a military system centered around highly sophisticated, efficient, and technical weapons systems. As early as 1957 this new character of the military was recognized. A report to President Eisenhower, based on a study of military personnel, stated that:

> Reduced to its simplest terms, the personnel problem appears to be a matter of quality as opposed to quantity. . . . It is foolish for the Armed Forces to obtain highly advanced weapons systems and not have men of sufficient competence to understand, operate, and maintain such equipment. . . . The solution here, of course, is not to draft more men to stand and look helplessly at the machinery.

As Representative Reuss of Wisconsin, pointed out last year, everything now indicates less and less need for a mass army and more and more need for a relatively smaller, highly trained, professional force. The draft is not designed to satisfy this new need, and, in fact, operates to frustrate it. The greater degree of weapons sophistication calls for a higher percentage of specialized personnel. This in turn requires greater professionalization which is obtained through extensive training and extended terms of service. But draftees, serving against their will, are in for 2 years and then inevitably leave before the months invested in specialized training can be effectively put to work.

Another consequence of the high turnover among draftees is the undermining of our military strength and the weakening of our national security. Gen. Lynn Smith has stated that 43 percent of the Army at any given time has less than 1 year's experience and, according to the general, the acknowledged basic problem of the Army today is too much personnel turbulence. By the time a unit is sufficiently experienced and able to operate as a team, the trained men leave, are replaced by green trainees and the cycle starts all over again.

It has been clearly demonstrated, I believe, that the current draft system does not allow the maximum amount of personal liberty; does not apply equally to all young men; and does not economically provide the type of personnel needed by the military.

President Johnson has proposed that the manpower requirements of the armed services be met through a lottery. Under this system, the necessary number of draftees would be selected on a random basis from a pool of draft-eligible 18-year-olds. Does this attempt to doctor the draft bring it any closer to meeting the criteria necessary for an effective military manpower procurement system?

First, this method does not alter the fact that forcing young men into military service—regardless of the procedure used in selecting who shall be drafted—still contradicts our traditional belief in the right of the individual to personal liberty and freedom from government interference. The lottery just makes this denial of liberty a little more arbitrary.

Second, this method of selecting who shall serve does not alleviate the basic injustice of the draft, but merely treats some of its symptoms. The lottery approach, if accompanied by other reforms, could reduce some of the inequities currently found in the deferment system and in the lack of uniform administration of the draft laws by the thousands of local draft boards. But it does not remedy the basic inequity of the draft; the injustice of forcing one man to serve while another is allowed his liberty. As Bruce Chapman questioned in his book "Wrong Man in Uniform," is injustice handed out by a machine any more tolerable than injustice handed out by other men? Chapman's strongest criticism of a lottery system "is that it would not come to grips with the new manpower facts of the nation and the military, that a smaller and smaller percentage of young men would be forced to sacrifice for the balance. Since pure chance, neither reasonable nor compassionate, would choose the draftee, the lottery would also be supremely callous, a dehumanizing, frivolous, Government-sponsored game of Russian roulette."

Finally, the lottery method of determining who shall serve in no way reduces the inefficiency or costliness of the draft, does not increase the quality of military personnel, and does not strengthen our national security.

The lottery approach is a patchwork proposal designed to cover some of the gaping holes in the fabric of military conscription but it does little to retailor the flaws in the basic design of the draft.

Let us measure one more method of military manpower recruitment against the criteria that has been established. Let us consider how well a voluntary system of meeting manpower needs meets the standards by which we judged —and rejected—the other manpower procurement systems. First, a volunteer system provides maximum individual liberty and freedom of choice. No one would be forced to serve in the Armed Forces against his will.

Second. A voluntary military would eliminate the inequities of the current draft system. Those men who assumed the burden of insuring our national security would do so willingly. Gone would be the injustices of the deferment system, and gone would be the inequities created by the lack of uniform policy in the nation's 4,000 local draft boards.

Third. The volunteer system of manpower recruitment must meet the criterion of providing for maximum national security and for the efficient and economical supplying of the necessary quantity and quality of men.

It is difficult to project with any accuracy the potential cost for a volunteer or professional armed forces. Even the Secretary of Defense is unable to estimate with any consistency the price tag of a volunteer military. His predictions have ranged from $4 to $20 billion.

In estimating the cost of a volunteer service, the increased expense of raised pay scales and improved benefits must be weighed against the economies that would result under this system. The report issued following the 1957 study of military personnel estimated that more realistic pay scales would increase enlistments and would allow a 10-percent cutback in maintenance technicians as higher morale and better training would reduce damage to technical equipment. The total possible savings estimated by this report, if its recommendations had been followed, were $2.8 billion in 1960 and $5 billion in 1962. These would have been substantial savings and strongly suggest that economies would be realized under an effective volunteer system.

Perhaps the largest economy of a volunteer military would be the reduced cost of high turnover. The current draftee turnover rate is nearly 95 percent while the turnover rate is about 15 percent for career men. If this reenlistment rate of 85 percent could be maintained in an all-volunteer force, the savings in the cost of training new inductees would be considerable. And, there is another side to the picture. We are spending 25 percent of our military effort to train men who do not stay. A reduction in trainees through lowered turnover rates would mean a corresponding reduction in the number of instructors and training facilities it is now necessary, and costly, to maintain. Further economies could be made through a reduction in the size of the military forces, and therefore, a reduction in the number of men necessary to train. A smaller armed service could be achieved by the substitution of civilians for military personnel in noncombatant positions. Representative Thomas Curtis, of Missouri, has estimated that it costs the Government $18,000 to keep one soldier for a year. Hiring a civilian to replace this soldier in such functions as storeroom clerk, maintenance man, or typist would be considerably less expensive.

The substitution of civilians for military personnel would not only lower costs but would reduce the size of the Armed Forces and thereby reduce the number of men necessary to recruit. Another step that should be taken to insure that a volunteer system of military manpower procurement was able to recruit the necessary number of volunteers, would be to accept the large number of young men who now try to volunteer and who would like a military career but who are currently rejected because of slight physical or educational deficiencies. Through additional and specialized training programs, these men could become productive members of the armed services.

The recruitment of the necessary quantity of men to meet military manpower needs would be further assured under a voluntary enlistment system because of the fewer servicemen that need to be replaced due to lowered turnover rates.

Finally, steps taken to increase the benefits and status of a military career and to make it competitive with opportunities in private industry, would attract increased numbers of volunteers.

A voluntary military recruitment program is not only economically feasible, and capable of producing the necessary number of recruits, it can also provide the quality of military personnel that is vital to the sophisticated and technical nature of the armed services. The lengthened periods of service would result in a better trained force more capable of operating complicated modern weapons. These career soldiers would take greater pride in their work, would function more efficiently and professionally, and as the foundation of our national defense system, they would increase our national security.

A voluntary armed services program, then, could meet the necessary criteria for an effective military manpower procurement system. But it must pass one more test. The critics of a voluntary military have stated that such a system would not be adequately flexible during times of crisis. I submit that it would be more flexible and, in conjunction with a strengthened Reserve and National Guard, would be better able to respond to an emergency situation than is the current draft system.

According to Gen. Lynn Smith, 43 percent of the Army at any given time has less than 1 year's experience. In an emergency situation are we willing to risk the possible consequences of committing these inexperienced troops? In the past, when confronted with crises that required a rapid buildup of military strength, the Defense Department has declined to use draftees but has called up the Reserve Forces. During the Korean war more than 600,000 World War II veterans were called back while 1,600,000 young men of draft age were not called. During the Berlin crisis, 150,000 reservists were called to active duty while the draft calls were enlarged only by several thousand. There would likely be much less reluctance to commit an experienced and well-trained armed service in times of crisis. A voluntary and professional military force, with a strengthened Reserve, could respond more quickly and effectively to a crisis than can the present system.

A volunteer military manpower recruitment system would work. But for such a system to be given a chance to prove its merit, we must dispel the myth that the draft, however undesirable, is inevitable. We must be willing to accept the challenges of new realities and have the foresight and confidence to accept logic over habit and reason over the retarding security of tradition.

A volunteer military is a workable alternative to conscription.

Questions for specimen speech analysis

1. What in your judgment, was Senator Hatfield's real purpose in making the speech? To what audience was he addressing his remarks?

2. Do you consider the topic worthy of consideration? Should the alternative Senator Hatfield proposed be considered?

3. What forms of reasoning did the senator use to support his plan? Was his reasoning sound?

4. What evidence did he offer to support his arguments? Did he employ any specific facts? If so, how effectively did he marshal them?

5. What motive appeals did he employ? Would you consider them worthy or unworthy? Effective or ineffective?

6. How was the speech organized? Was there a clear, relevant introduction and a strong, moving conclusion? Was the structure unified around a central theme? Were the parts clearly related to each other? Were there smooth transitions between the divisions of the speech?

7. Was his language appropriate for the purpose, occasion, speaker and audience? Was the language clear and compelling? Were the sentences well-constructed? How would you describe Senator Hatfield's style in this speech?

THREE

Ceremonial occasions: inspiring

Commemorative, commencement, and inaugural speeches

Purpose and occasion

Carlyle Marney, speaking to my graduating class at college said that commencement speakers were much like the chorus of frogs in Aristophanes' play; what they said did not mean anything, but they seemed necessary for the performance. There are a number of occasions on which speechmaking is traditional and expected and for which speechmaking is a central part of the ceremony itself.

If it is true that the speech of the day is an essential part of these ceremonies, it is equally true that the speech is oriented toward and focused on the ceremony, rather than on a subject, the speaker, or the audience. These speeches are occasion-centered; both subject and treatment are dictated by the occasion, by the nature of the ceremony itself.

Generally, the purpose of these ceremonial speeches is to impress the audience. (Is it not the very nature of ritual to take concepts and dramatize them for audiences? Does it not stand to reason, then, that the address part of a ritual should have the same central purpose?) But what is it to impress? It is to move, to touch, to affect the spirit; it is to engrave an idea on the mind. We often say, "He made a profound impression on me," or "What he said was very impressive." We mean that, in some way, the speaker captured our imagination and left an indelible mark on our memory. In ceremonial speeches, you have the task of eliciting that kind of response from your hearers.

Speeches to impress are given on a variety of occasions. Although the ceremonies are different, the speeches have a great deal in common. On commemorative occasions you usually pay tribute; at commencement and installation ceremonies you deliver a charge; and at inaugurations you deliver a pledge. There are many kinds of commemorative occasions: memorial services, testimonial dinners, anniversaries, and dedications, for example.

In each case, however, your function is to deepen the appreciation and respect of the listeners for the person, persons, event, institution, or monument. You must impress them with the worth of the ones to whom you pay tribute. In eulogies and testimonial speeches, you will emphasize the traits, qualities, and contributions of the person you and the audience gather to honor. At graduations, you will usually address yourself to the graduates and try to impress them (and other listeners) with the importance and value of their achievement and the responsibilities that achievement imposes. When you are inaugurated, you will probably deliver a brief address to impress your audience with your vision, your commitment, and your program.

Remember, when you are called upon to speak at one of these occasions, you will stand out best by fitting into the whole ceremony, and you will make the most favorable impression for yourself by focusing attention on the person or event you are there to honor.

Preparation

Precisely because speakers at ceremonies often say little worth noting or long remembering, you should feel challenged to prepare carefully and to speak well. In these speeches, substance is uncommon and eloquence is rare, but that fact should stimulate you all the more to thorough preparation.

Topics. The topics for ceremonial occasions are more or less dictated by the occasion itself, but there is an infinite variety possible in your approach and treatment. The central idea of a commemorative speech will probably be "_____ is worthy of praise (or honor, tribute, or emulation)." If you are speaking at a memorial service, you certainly cannot talk about somebody other than the one in whose memory the group meets; if you are speaking at an anniversary, it would not be fitting to center your remarks around observing some other event or celebration; if you are speaking at the dedication of a building named for Hubert Humphrey, it would hardly be appropriate for you to spend your time lauding the achievements of Robert Kennedy. The occasion will limit your subject.

Although it is possible to speak on a topic unrelated directly to the occasion, it is uncommon and generally undesirable to do so. President Kennedy used commencement occasions to announce and advance important public policies, but he did so knowing that he had a nation-wide, even worldwide, audience. For most of us, it is better to confine ourselves at graduations to addressing the graduates, their relatives and friends. The central theme of your commencement address might be "The graduates of _____ merit our respect (congratulations or admiration) and have assumed certain responsibilities." Or it might be "The graduates of _____ have earned this award and now face new duties." In any case, fashion the address to the nature of the school and the graduating class; fit your speech specifically to them.

Inaugural addresses give you more freedom in the choice of a topic than do most other ceremonial speeches. The principal theme will likely be "I pledge to carry out my duties and my program," but the real topic will be your concept of your duties and your program— whatever that may be.

Materials. Speeches for the occasions being discussed are, as we have said, speeches to impress the audience with the worth or significance of someone or something. But where can you look for materials with which to do the impressing? There are two principal sources: your audience and your subject. You must analyze your audience to discover what it will consider worthy of respect, praise, or honor, and you must analyze the subject to discover the elements that fit the audience's criteria of worthiness.

Audience Analysis. Ideals, values, aspirations, and traditions vary from group to group and from culture to culture. What one audience might approve, another from a different background might wholeheartedly condemn. If you seek to pay tribute, to deliver a charge, or issue a pledge, you must do so on the basis of those sentiments the audience already holds.

Much of this advice, you will readily admit, is just common sense.

You would not get up before a group of Young Republicans gathered at a testimonial dinner to honor Barry Goldwater and praise him for his great contributions to uniting the Democratic Party. You would surely laud him in terms of the ideals and values Young Republicans share with Mr. Goldwater. Nor would you expect an American President speaking at a West Point or Annapolis commencement to justify our military intervention in some conflict on the basis that aggression on our part is justified; the President would have to defend his policy and his actions on the basis of traditional American ideals (among which aggression is not included). And no matter how much a President may intend to modify social and economic patterns, he will not announce in his inaugural address that he plans to lead us toward socialism; the word, at least, is outside traditional American aspirations.

To discover on what bases you can impress them, you should analyze your audience in terms of their ideals, values, aspirations, and traditions.

Ideals are standards of excellence. Ask yourself, "What would this audience believe to be the perfect one of its or his type?" If you are praising a Democrat to fellow-Democrats, you would want to determine what they would consider the perfect Democrat; if you are honoring an alumnus at a class reunion, you would decide what the listeners would respect as the ideal alumnus; if you are paying tribute to the fraternity sweetheart at the annual sweetheart dance, you would think of those attributes the brothers, alumni, and dates believe characteristic of the quintessence of sweethearts. On a rating scale of excellence, what would these hearers deem perfection?

Not everyone can be praised in terms of ideals, but most can be praised in terms of the audience's values. Values are estimates of worth, usefulness, or importance; they are those things and those attributes that are worthy of esteem for their own sake. Ask yourself, "What characteristics does this audience respect which need no justification apart from their own existence?" "What would this audience honor without question or reservation?" "What does it hold dear?" "What does it think worthwhile, noble, good?" "What does it believe important?" "What does it prize, and what does it think valuable?" Your task, of course, is to identify the value system of your listeners and identify that which you seek to honor with those values. Do they honor courage? Then praise your hero for his fearlessness. Do they value peace? Then laud him for his contributions to international understanding. Do they hold virtue estimable? Then comment on the fact you are proud she is someone you can respect. At a meeting of the Mafia, you would be more likely to praise loyalty than honesty, and at a meeting of the church auxiliary, you would be more likely to speak of a benefactor's generosity than of his alcoholism. On a rating scale of worthiness, determine what the audience would consider better rather than worse.

In addition to ideals and values, you should also analyze the listeners in terms of aspirations. Aspirations are steadfast desires, goals, or ends. They are the hopes, dreams, and ambitions of your audience. Ask yourself, "What are these people aiming toward?" "What do they hope to achieve?" "What do they want to see accomplished?" "Would they rejoice to see something done, and if so, what is it?" "What do they dream of for themselves and their children?" In his first inaugural address, Franklin Roosevelt recognized the deepest aspirations of the American people at the time and spoke to them; they hoped for reassurance, leadership, action, and economic improvement, and he addressed himself to those yearnings. Commencement speakers as well as inaugural speakers should deal with the aspirations of the audience. If you are called on to speak at a graduation, think in terms of the expectations and goals of the graduates and their parents. Those ambitions and desires will provide you with material for your address.

Through analysis of your audience, you may also find speech material in their traditions. Traditions are those beliefs and practices that have been handed down in the group from their predecessors. They are long established and generally accepted customs and methods of procedure. Traditions may not have the force of law in all groups, but they certainly do exert a strong influence. The majority of people appear to be rather conservative, in the sense that they hesitate not only to alter but also to contravene traditional practices and beliefs. Suicide is a respected tradition in some cultures, but not in our own. In a eulogy for a man who died by his own hand, you would not be expected to praise him for flaunting our customs. If you were called on to give a speech of tribute for those arrested in a campaign of civil disobedience, could you find any American tradition to use to honor them? You might trace the tradition of "obeying a higher law" both in the Bible ("We must obey God rather than men," for example) and in American history (the Boston Tea Party, the underground rail-

road, and the demonstrations of the suffragettes, for example). But I
would remind you that certain of these examples would be more effective with some American audiences than with others! In any case,
there is a tradition in this country of disobeying laws thought to be
unjust to which you could turn for supporting material. You ought to
recognize that we have many traditions, many of them somewhat contrary to each other, and you must select those traditions that will serve
to impress your audience most favorably. Be careful in selecting the
traditions to which you will appeal. Most American Presidents, at their
inauguration, seem to feel compelled to invoke the aid of the Deity
(because of America's strong religious tradition), but that is one tradition you might not need to call upon if you are being inaugurated as
president of the P.T.A. of a public school.

Clearly, then, the audience will provide you with a wealth of material for your speech. After you have determined the ideals, values,
aspirations, and traditions your hearers hold in common, you will have
to select those that are most appropriate to your purpose and your
topic. You cannot use them all. Applying good judgment and good
taste, choose those sentiments that will most deeply move and most
favorably impress.

Subject Analysis. After studying your audience for materials you can
use, you must analyze the subject of your discourse to discover materials to include when you construct your speech. If your subject is a
person, you should study his life, work, and contributions. If possible,
interview people who knew him and worked with him and ask his
friends and relatives for materials they might be willing to share with
you and your audience. If your subject is an organization or a movement, study its history and development. Use primary sources wherever possible. Read the records and talk with the officers. Check newspaper accounts of the various periods. And if the group published
anything, get it and read it. Get firsthand information if you can. If
you are speaking at a dedication ceremony, you should certainly find
out about the origin of the monument, the development of the idea,
and the means of bringing it into being; you should also know as much
as you can about the one for whom it is a memorial. If your speech
is delivered at an installation, you should be familiar with the organization, the duties of the officers, and the qualifications of the people
being installed. There is no substitute for specific information in any
speech; a commencement address is certainly no exception. Every-

thing you can learn about the school or institution, its history, its traditions, its purpose, and about the graduates, their backgrounds, their records, their expectations, and their aspirations, may provide interesting and useful supporting material.

If you think of research as more than a reading assignment in a library, then I am recommending that you do an extensive effort at research on your topic. Specifically, I would suggest that you look for allusions, comparisons, contrasts, examples, factual information, illustrations and anecdotes, sound reasoning, and quotations.

Allusions. Allusions are indirect references to other works of literature. Without quoting directly and without necessarily citing the original source of the idea or phrase, you may use wording that echoes familiar passages. Adlai Stevenson drew on a number of sources—the Bible, Greek and Roman mythology, Shakespeare and many other great writers, and history. The allusions enriched his speeches but escaped many in his audiences who were not familiar with the original sources. John Kennedy was another who drew on literature and history for materials for his addresses.

Although it was hardly a tribute, the speaker who said, "The State Department is the President's right hand, the Defense Department is his left hand, and both are following the Biblical injunction" was using an allusion. He referred, without mentioning it, of course, to Jesus' statement about secrecy in giving alms that the left hand should not know what the right hand is doing. To be effective, the allusion must be immediately clear to the audience. This allusion, for example, would make no sense to people who are illiterate biblically. If you know that your listeners are well acquainted with a particular body of literature, search that literature for materials to which you can refer.

Comparisons. While studying your topic, you may discover certain similarities between the person, organization, or event you plan to discuss and other, more familiar persons, institutions, or events. If so, explore the likenesses further. You may find material to augment and amplify the impression you seek to give. The more unusual, fresh, or thought-provoking the comparison, the better. Comparing graduates of a school of nursing with Florence Nightingale is hardly startling and, therefore, hardly moving and impressive. The secret of effective use of comparison lies in the ability to see relationships. Like the poet, you should be able to see similarities that are not immediately and universally obvious. In a commemorative address, you might tell what the man you seek to praise has in common with someone (perhaps in a different field) the audience greatly admires; in a commencement address, you might compare the challenges facing the graduates with challenges faced and conquered by others they would respect; in an inaugural address, you might compare your program with a program of which the audience already approves. Do not strain to establish likenesses, but rather let them be suggested to you by the topic itself. If the subject does bring to your mind some similarities, explore them.

Contrasts. Contrasts are simply the reverse side of comparisons; instead of likenesses, they are differences. The speaker who said, "Unlike Christopher Columbus, who did not know where he was going or where he had been when he got back, the man we honor tonight has known exactly what he was doing since he began to lead us. We did not arrive at our new world of experience through any accident. . . ." was using contrast to impress his audience with the man's distinctive qualities. One commencement speaker contrasted the problems facing graduates at the turn of this century with those facing graduates today. Perhaps you can think of other appropriate contrasts for commencement or inaugural addresses.

Examples. Examples are specific instances cited to support or clarify an idea. The word means literally "something taken out," a sample that is typical of the larger concept. If you wish to demonstrate a person's generosity, you could cite instances of his liberal giving to establish the point. Examples are not ordinarily amplified; they are simply enumerated or listed.

Illustrations and Anecdotes. Illustrations are expanded examples; they are stories told to make a point clear or vivid. To be effective in impressing, the narratives must contain specific, concrete details and must be worded in vivid, colorful, and action-packed language. Illustrations give a speech "human interest"; they clothe abstract ideas and impersonal generalizations in human terms; they bring truths home to us by relating them to experiences we understand. To accomplish its purpose, the story must be related through accurate, believable, graphic description. It must be presented realistically; the narrative must "ring true."

Remember, in choosing illustrations for your speech, each illustration must serve a particular purpose; it must **illustrate** some principle or some concept. Do not tell stories just to tell stories. Tell them only to make some point clear and memorable. If you are preparing a eulogy, decide which aspects of the person's character you wish to conjure up for your listeners, and then select stories from the person's life to illustrate those specific characteristics. If you plan to use stories in your commencement address to make your assertions more meaningful, select stories clearly related to the points and easily understood by the audience. Illustrations must be within the range of experience and comprehension of the listeners if they are to clarify rather than mystify, interest rather than bore.

Factual Information. One source of supporting material you might well explore is factual information—deeds, acts, events, or states. Things that have happened, things that were, things that are: these bits of reality form excellent buttressing material, even in speeches whose primary purpose is to impress. Truth can be most impressive! Tell it "like it is."

Factual support consists of data (bits, pieces, fragments) of experience perceived by someone through his senses and reported. Factual information is the result of reports of reception of stimuli through one of the five senses—sight, hearing, taste, smell, or touch. Facts, then, are verifiable; presumably anyone in full control of his senses would have perceived the same thing had he been present. A fact, unlike a judgment or conclusion, may be said to be true. What we observe and experience through our senses we can test or verify by checking the experience of others. Facts tell us what actually happened or what actually existed, and these facts should be clearly distinguished from our interpretation and conclusions with regard to them.

Facts are appropriate in any kind of speech. Do not overlook them when preparing ceremonial speeches.

Sound reasoning. Reasoning is difficult to define. Perhaps it is best to say simply that it is the drawing of inferences or conclusions from facts and assumptions. It involves moving from one statement to another statement (the conclusion) by means of a logical leap in which we assume that the move is warranted. Sound reasoning has to do with moving to conclusions in a logically justifiable way.

You will not only use factual information in your speeches; you will also interpret that information and draw conclusions from it. To be impressive, your thinking must be clear and valid. Your purpose in these ceremonial speeches is not to present arguments to persuade, but to expound judgments to impress. Facts will be reported, but judgments must be explained. Be certain that your interpretation is logical, so it will be acceptable to your audience.

Quotations. The last source of supporting material is the use of another's words to underscore your point. Speakers use quotations to emphasize, amplify, and restate an idea. You may, in your preparation, discover a passage that expresses your concept better than you can. Perhaps the writer used beautiful, memorable, moving language; perhaps the writer put the truth unusually sharply, concisely, and clearly; perhaps the writer clothed the point in sensitive poetry.

Whatever its distinctive literary quality, you may wish to include it in your own speech. If it is clearly related to the point you are making, if it contributes to your purpose of impressing, if you give proper credit to the writer or speaker whose words you are utilizing, and if you can introduce the quotation smoothly, then feel free to use the quoted material.

One warning about the use of quotations: do not precede them with the awkward announcement, "quote," and conclude them with the equally gauche word, "unquote." You can acknowledge the use of another man's language through an introductory sentence, clause, or phrase. Unless you read aloud all marks of punctuation and say "comma," "period," or "exclamation mark," you should not read aloud the quotation marks. Instead, you could use the phrase, "According to Homer Kleep," or the clause, "As Sophie Glutz observed," or the sentence, "Seymour Kleerly expressed the idea in his own piquant style," or any of the countless variations you may devise as a preface.

Organization. After you have selected your topic and gathered your materials through analysis of the audience and the subject, you face the task of putting the materials into an organized framework. This framework forms the structure of your address, which must be logical in its arrangement and easy for listeners to follow.

In discussing the topic, we mentioned the necessity of deciding on a single sentence that summarizes the entire speech. This central theme is the first step in arranging your materials, and its selection is a crucial step. Unless you decide specifically what total impression you want to leave with your audience, you will have no criterion for inclusion or exclusion of materials and for determining the order in which materials should come in the speech.

After you have decided on your central theme, you are ready to select the major divisions of the body of your speech. If your central

theme is "_____ is worthy of honor," your major divisions will probably be reasons why he is worthy. If your central idea is "The graduates of _____ merit our respect and have assumed certain responsibilities," you will have two major divisions: (1) "They merit our respect," and (2) "They have assumed certain responsibilities." In this
case, you will have to subdivide each of your major divisions, the first
into reasons they merit our respect and the second into each of the
major responsibilities you think they have assumed. If your essential
message is summarized in the statement "I pledge to carry out my
duties and my program," you will logically have two major divisions
(each subdivided, of course): (1) "I pledge to carry out my duties," and
(2) "I pledge to carry out my program." It is clear that, if your central
theme is properly worded, construction of the major divisions of the
body will logically follow.

The central idea should force you to speak on one topic and one
alone, guaranteeing unity in the speech, and the properly selected
divisions should force you to keep the various parts of the body related and balanced, insuring coherence and appropriate emphasis.

Only after you have settled upon the structure of the body of the
speech should you decide on the conclusion and introduction. The
conclusion should bring the entire address to an impressive climax.
Whether it is a summary, a recapitulation of your major points, a
quotation, a final illustration, or an emotional appeal, the conclusion
should be brief, fitting, and stirring. Therefore, the conclusion must
be prepared carefully and worded well. The conclusion leaves a final
and often lasting impression on your audience; it must "pack a
punch." In the introduction, you must gain the attention, interest, and
goodwill of your listeners and focus their attention on your theme. If
possible, you should establish some common ground with the audience and, because the occasion is so important in these speeches of
ceremony, relate the subject to the occasion. The introduction should
be only long enough to accomplish these purposes. Like the conclusion, it should be thoughtfully prepared and carefully worded.

Adaptation, style, and other distinctives

Since the speaking is an integral part of the ceremony, the occasion
demands high standards of eloquence. Significant ideas should be
presented in esthetically pleasing language. Commemorations, dedi-

cations, installations, graduations, and inaugurations are not times for trotting out truisms garbed in worn-out, colorless words.

True it is that you may not say much that is new, but you can present what you have to say in a fresh, new, and memorable way. Your style should be lofty without grandiloquence, forceful without ostentation, imaginative without floweriness, precise without pedantry, simple without condescension, carefully constructed without euphuism. Your words should so intensify the ideas that they will be etched into your hearers' memories. Your aim is to choose language that will leave an indelible impression on your audience.

But what kind of language makes a favorable and lasting impression? Words that are clear, appropriate, and vivid, sentences that are straightforward and varied, and rhetorical devices that enhance the dignity, beauty, and effectiveness of the address make such an impression on audiences.

Words. Your words should be clear. Choose words your listeners will know and understand. Words are neither for display nor attack; they should not dazzle or confuse the audience. Remember that your purpose is to communicate ideas, and your words must be chosen with this fact in mind. A speaker who failed to understand this principle said: "During this joyous Advent season, as you peruse the advertising in periodicals and other mass media of communication and go your peripatetic way among the shops, I trust that you will pause to ponder the more profound essence of meaning inherent in Yuletide." How much more effective he would have been had he said: "This year, I hope you will take time out from watching TV commercials, reading newspaper ads, and shopping for gifts to give some thought to the real meaning of Christmas."

Choose words that are not only clear to your audience but are also appropriate for the subject and occasion. Ceremonies are usually rather formal occasions; slang, hip language, common or coarse talk is out of place. Avoid the ungrammatical or the vulgar. In a commemorative speech, you would hardly be expected to say, "He had a lot of dough." You would be more likely to say, "He was a man of great wealth." If you were praising a person for his loyalty to friends, you surely would not proclaim that "he never ratted on his buddies!" Use good taste and good judgment in selecting words. There are various levels of language usage; choose that level of wording that befits the time, the place, and the purpose of the gathering.

Your words should also be vivid and arresting. Good taste and good judgment do not imply dullness! Your words should have life and color. Avoid overworked words and hackneyed expressions. Clichés bore audiences; arresting language holds attention and captures imagination. If you want to turn off the mind of every listener, imitate the speaker who said: "It is a pleasure and a privilege to be here today. That generous introduction by my old friend warmed my heart. It is always a joy to be with you, but I feel a special thrill today at being asked to share in this glorious occasion. . . ." The speaker who says to high school graduates, "If you do not remember another thing from this speech, remember . . ." hardly deserves to be remembered at all, and speakers who urge graduates to "make this world a better place in which to live" deserve to live in a worse place than this world for inflicting that cliché on us again! Alan Monroe, in an appendix of the fourth edition of **Principles and Types of Speech,** gives some lists of trite expressions you should avoid. His list is only a beginning, but you can add to it.

Speakers seem unusually tempted in ceremonial speeches to fall back on "the tried and true" expressions. In preparing these speeches, you should exercise extreme caution to be certain that your own addresses are not filled with clichés.

Sentences. Exercise care not only in choosing words but also in constructing sentences. Remember that your listeners must understand your thought on the basis of one hearing; they are not readers who can go back and reread passages they did not comprehend the first time. Your sentences, then, must be direct and to the point. Even long sentences must be instantly clear and the relationships among the ideas easy to grasp.

Variety is another principle to keep in mind in the construction of sentences. Vary sentences in length, in form, and in type. Use simple, compound, and complex sentences when they are appropriate, and in addition to statements, use questions, imperatives, and exclamations. Do not allow your sentences to fall into a monotonous pattern. The well-turned phrase and the well-constructed sentence are essential marks of good oral style.

Stylistic Devices. If you would develop impressive style, you should also give some attention to stylistic devices. Of these devices, imagery is by far the most important, but you should also know about some of the others and use them when they are appropriate for you, your audience, and your purpose.

Imagery. Through our five senses we receive impressions of the world around us; we perceive the world, we experience it, by sensing it. Our conceptions are determined by what we see, hear, taste, smell, and touch. But your listeners cannot see the antibodies form in the scientist's test tube, they cannot hear the roar of the artillery, they cannot taste the bitter hemlock, they cannot smell the smoke of the gutted building, they cannot feel the pain of the hero's wounds. How, then, can they conceive of them and respond? Through your words, you must conjure up these sensations in the minds of your hearers. Your language must stir the imaginations of your audience and produce in them mental imitations of the sensory response. Language that stimulates this mental representation is called imagery.

Impressing requires vivid description, and vivid description can be achieved primarily through language that appeals to the senses. To give force and intensity to your ideas, you must use words that make your audience feel it is experiencing firsthand what you describe. An eyewitness to the horrors of war described "a string of ears hacked from the heads of terrified prisoners that decorates the wall of the government's military headquarters." Can you see the grim trophy? Can you see the terror-struck victims? Can you feel the chop of the machete blade? Does the following passage from a newspaperman's account stir up mental images?

> "I got me a VC, man. I got at least two of them bastards." The exultant cry followed a 10-second burst of automatic weapon fire yesterday, and the dull crump of a grenade exploding underground. The Marines ordered a Vietnamese corporal to go down into the grenade-blasted hole to pull out their victims. The victims were three children between 11 and 14—two boys and a girl. Their bodies were riddled with bullets.... "Oh, my God," a young Marine exclaimed. "They're all kids. . . ."[1]

In addition to image-producing words used in description, the major forms of imagery are metaphor and simile.

Metaphor. An implied comparison, a metaphor is a figure of speech in which one thing is spoken of as if it were something else. A metaphor results from employing a word or words ordinarily used of one thing to apply to another. They are images which, though not literally accurate, suggest a relationship the speaker holds to be valid. The word **metaphor** means literally "to carry over" and implies that unusual terms are being transferred to some object. To be effective at using metaphors, you must be able to see resemblances and relation-

[1] New York **Herald Tribune**, August 3, 1965.

ships that escape ordinary notice. Metaphors ornament and enrich a speech when they are used well; used badly, they can become ridiculous.

In World War II, General Rommel was called "the desert fox," an interesting metaphor based on his craftiness and expertise in tactics. President Franklin Roosevelt promised to lead the American people down "a new and untrod path," a less fortunate metaphor for two reasons: (1) comparing a course of action to a path is hardly new and (2) a path is not worn without treading.

Three dangers of which you should beware are: (1) worn-out metaphors, (2) overdone metaphors, and (3) mixed metaphors.

Metaphors can lose their effectiveness through overuse. Please do not tell graduates they are "building for the future" or they have "laid a good foundation for their higher education." Nor should you refer to their "horizons," to "opening windows of opportunity," or to "shouldering the burdens of responsibility." Someone has said all those things a few times before. If you want to express the ideas that were once conveyed by those expressions, find some new, fresh ways to state them.

Metaphors can be developed in such detail and pursued for so long that they become disastrously tedious or hilariously funny. One of my students, Michael Felty, in a delightful spoof of cliché-ridden speeches of tribute gives an excellent example of overdone metaphors.

> Eastern Kentucky University Infirmary has a very nice staff. With its doctor and its staff, it comforts us. This is one institution where the milk of human kindness has not gone sour. Indeed, its cup runneth over, because the staff of our great infirmary is the cream of the crop. If a student butters them up sufficiently, he will get decent service.

Mixed metaphors result from combining two or more inconsistent metaphors into a single expression. While Secretary of Agriculture, Henry A. Wallace said, "The butter folks are on the hot spot" and produced a gooey bit of imagery. He also confused those familiar with anatomy with this mixed metaphor: "Young people have been the backbone of every strong-arm movement in Europe!" If you are going to use metaphors, use one image at a time.

In spite of the dangers of misuse, metaphors remain the most important single stylistic device and, when well done, exemplify the most beautiful use of language. Note the metaphors in the conclusion of John F. Kennedy's speech before the September 25, 1961 meeting of the U.N. General Assembly:

But however close we sometimes seem to that dark and final abyss, let no man of peace and freedom despair. For he does not stand alone. If we can in every land and office look beyond our own shores and ambitions, then surely the age will dawn in which the strong are just and the weak secure, and the peace is preserved.

Simile. A metaphor, as we have seen, is an implied comparison made by substituting the compared idea for the one to be illuminated or illustrated; a simile, on the other hand, is an explicit comparison announced by **like, as,** or some other comparable word. "My love is a rose" would be a metaphor, but "My love is like a rose" or "My beloved is as lovely as a rose" would be similes. Both devices are used to add interest, freshness, and beauty to the address.

You may decide for yourself the effectiveness of this simile from a student's "Tribute to a Failure": "Like Icarus, he dared too much and aimed too high. . . ." Martin Luther King on more than one occasion has quoted these Biblical similes: "Let justice roll down like waters and righteousness like a mighty stream." Would the imagery be meaningful to modern audiences if a speaker presented this ironic simile: "as warm as Caligula and as kind as Nero"? And how would you evaluate this symbolic statement of Clarence Darrow's frustration? "I have stood here for three months [during the Leopold and Loeb trial] as one might stand at the ocean trying to sweep back the tide."

If the image is graphic, a simile can be an effective device for impressing an audience.

Direct address. Talking to your audience directly can assist you in communication. Using personal pronouns **I, you,** and **we** creates the feeling that you are talking with the audience rather than to them or before them. Using the personal approach of "you and I" instead of the impersonal "one" gives the impression that you consider yourself part of the group and that you are not talking down to your listeners.

President Franklin Roosevelt was identified with his customary salutation, "My friends," and that form of direct address was appropriate for him. Find ways of addressing your hearers that befit the audience and occasion and that seem pleasant and natural to you.

Apostrophe. The word **apostrophe** comes to us from two Greek words meaning "to turn from" and refers to the device of turning from addressing the audience directly to speak directly to some individual or some thing, either present or absent. Governor Frank Clement was using this figure of speech when he suddenly turned from his audience and exclaimed, "How long, O America, how long. . . ." I would hesitate to use the device; most contemporary American audiences, I believe, would think it "corny."

Personification. If you speak of a thing or an abstraction as if it were a person, you are using the variety of metaphor called personification. St. Paul talked to death as if it had the attributes of a personal enemy when he said, "Where, Death, is your victory?" It may not have occurred to the young man writing the eulogy that he was using personification when he wrote "He is gone and the nation mourns," because we accept the device of attributing human traits to objects, groups, qualities, and ideas without much reservation. Perhaps, after all, we commonly think of things and abstractions as having personalities and the figure of speech is but a natural outgrowth of that thinking.

Parallelism. Parallelism is the stylistic device based on similarity in either idea or structure, of successive phrases, clauses, or sentences. The word, which we got from Greek, means literally "beside one another"; things that are parallel lie alongside each other and match each other. In rhetoric, things that are parallel correspond to each other, either in concept or in construction.

Hebrew poetry offers some of the most beautiful examples of parallelism. Analyze the Psalms or the Lord's Prayer and you will discover the parallel pattern: the second phrase repeats the first phrase in other words. Just note these few examples:

> The Lord is my shepherd;
> I shall not want. (Psalms 23:1 RSV)

> The earth is the Lord's and the fulness thereof,
> The world and those who dwell therein. (Psalms 24:1 RSV)

> When I look at thy heavens, the work of thy fingers,
> The moon and the stars which thou hast established;
> What is man that thou art mindful of him,
> And the son of man that thou dost care for him? (Psalms 8:3, 4 RSV)

> Thy kingdom come,
> Thy will be done
> On earth as it is in heaven. (Matthew 6:10 RSV)

Although parallel ideas may be used in speeches, parallel construction is more common. Parallelism gives grace and balance to style; it lends elegance and dignity to your addresses. No one in recent times has used parallel structure more effectively than John F. Kennedy.

That device was characteristic of his distinctive style, and every speech was filled with multitudes of excellent examples. He used parallel words, phrases, clauses, and sentences in an almost endless variety.

To the graduating class at West Point in June 1962, President Kennedy said:

> Korea has not been the only battle ground since the end of the Second World War. Men have fought and died in Malaya, in Greece, in the Philippines, in Algeria and Cuba and Cyprus, and almost continuously on the Indochinese Peninsula. No nuclear retaliation has been considered appropriate. No nuclear weapons have been fired. This is another type of war, new in its intensity, ancient in its origin—war by guerrillas, subversives, insurgents, assassins; war by ambush instead of by combat, by infiltration instead of aggression, seeking victory by eroding and exhausting the enemy instead of engaging him.[2]

Later the same year, at Rice University, President Kennedy used parallelism to greet his audience:

> . . . We meet at a college noted for knowledge, in a city noted for progress, in a state noted for strength, and we stand in need of all three, for we meet in an hour of change and challenge, in a decade of hope and fear, in an age of both knowledge and ignorance. The greater our knowledge increases, the greater our ignorance unfolds.[3]

Parallelism is not only esthetically pleasing; it is memorable and impressive. Every schoolchild remembers Abraham Lincoln's parallel phrases, "of the people, by the people, and for the people." And even after so many years a listener is impressed with the recording of President Franklin Roosevelt's Declaration of War speech in which he piled up the parallel sentences:

> Yesterday the Japanese Government also launched an attack against Malaya.
>
> Last night Japanese forces attacked Hong Kong.
>
> Last night Japanese forces attacked Guam.
>
> Last night Japanese forces attacked the Philippine Islands.
>
> Last night the Japanese attacked Wake Island.
>
> And this morning the Japanese attacked Midway Island.

[2] John F. Kennedy, "What the Coming Army Officer Will Need," **The Burden and the Glory** (New York: Harper & Row, 1964), 240.
[3] Ibid, 241–242.

Parallelism, because of its grace, is especially appropriate for cere-monial speeches. Overdone, it seems affected, artificial, and high-flown, but used with judgment and taste, it lifts the style to match the occasion.

Antithesis. Another device useful in enhancing your style is anti-thesis, expressing in two successive phrases, clauses, or sentences a contrastive or opposite idea. The contrast may be expressed in the not-this-but-that formula or it may occur without such an explicit announcement.

President John F. Kennedy used antithesis effectively in his Inau-gural Address. His opening sentence, "We observe today not a victory of party but a celebration of freedom . . . ," is a good example. Another is: "We shall not always expect to find them [developing nations] sup-porting our view. But we shall always hope to find them strongly sup-porting their own freedom. . . ." His most memorable use of antithesis, of course, is: "And so, my fellow Americans, ask not what your coun-try can do for you; ask what you can do for your country." And to that antithesis, he added in parallel form a second: "My fellow citizens of the world, ask not what America will do for you, but what together we can do for the freedom of man."

Without the cue words "not" and "but," antitheses may be con-structed by joining two contrastive clauses, such as "One must in-crease; the other must decrease." Another example might be, "Some may prefer bitterness; I prefer brotherhood." Note that the structure is similar in the two clauses, but the ideas are either contrary or contradictory.

Climactic order. One technique for increasing interest and impres-siveness is to build a sequence of ideas in ascending order of im-portance or excitement. The series should reach its climax in the final phrase, clause, or sentence, with intensity developing progressively in each step to the last. Julius Caesar's "I came; I saw; I conquered" illustrates climactic order, as does the variation used by a Western Kentucky University debater, "Our opponents' position seems to be: 'We came; we saw: we concurred.' " Three weeks after his inauguration, President Kennedy spoke to a group of businessmen, many of whom thought his administration unfriendly to business, and used climactic order to build to the point he wished to make: "Whatever past dif-ferences may have existed, we seek more than an attitude of truce, more than a treaty; we seek the spirit of a full-fledged alliance. . . ."

Epigrams. In the speech to impress, you are chiefly saying the familiar in a new, fresh way. If your address is to be memorable (in the sense of being **worth** remembering and of actually remaining in the minds of your hearers) you must use phrases constructed so well they lodge in the memories of the listeners. Terse, pointed, pithy statements are called epigrams. They are usually the briefest and cleverest way of putting the idea. Most folk sayings (such as "A penny saved is a penny earned") are epigrams and have been preserved because they are easily remembered. Do not rely on ready-made epigrams; construct your own. Here are a few examples from the speeches of President Kennedy:

> We offer a special pledge: to convert our good words into good deeds. . . .
>
> Any dangerous spot is tenable if men—brave men—will make it so.
>
> We cannot negotiate with those who say, "What's mine is mine, and what's yours is negotiable."
>
> Peace and freedom do not come cheap. . . .

Refrain. As I have repeatedly stressed, style is most important in ceremonial speeches. At its best, such speaking is almost poetic, and you will probably have observed by now that several of the stylistic devices appropriate for these addresses are common to poetry as well. Heightened imagery, personification, parallelism, and antithesis, for example, are all characteristic of poetry. The last stylistic device we are going to consider is also typical of poetry: the use of refrain, which is the repetition of an idea at intervals for emphasis and effect.

If the repeated phrase "packs a punch" (or if you prefer, has a strong emotive appeal), the refrain may add greatly to the impressiveness of the address. Martin Luther King's speech delivered at the march on Washington is usually called his "I-Have-A-Dream" speech, because everyone was struck by his use of that sentence as a recurring theme. Senator Mike Mansfield, in his eulogy for President Kennedy delivered in the rotunda of the United States Capitol, used a touching refrain five times in the course of his brief address: "And so she took a ring from her finger and placed it in his hands." One of the most impressive of President Kennedy's own ceremonial speeches was his address in the Rudolph Wilde Platz in West Berlin. In the introduction of that speech, he used a refrain with great effectiveness:

There are many people in the world who really don't understand, or say they don't, what is the great issue between the free world and the Communist world. Let them come to Berlin. There are some who say that Communism is the wave of the future. Let them come to Berlin. And there are some who say in Europe and elsewhere we can work with the Communists. Let them come to Berlin. And there are even a few who say that it is true that Communism is an evil system, but it permits us to make economic progress. "Lasst sie nach Berlin kommen!"[4]

Presentation

There are, as you know, four methods of delivering speeches, and you must choose among them the one most suitable for you and your audience. The first, impromptu speaking, has nothing to commend it for a ceremonial occasion. Worthy sentiments expressed in lofty language do not come to you on the spur of the moment. Impressing requires careful, thoughtful preparation. But you may want to weigh the advantages and disadvantages of the other three modes of presentation.

Extemporaneous delivery. This method of presentation leaves nothing except the actual wording of the speech to the moment of delivery. The topic is carefully chosen, the central idea painstakingly phrased, the materials thoroughly researched, the structure of the speech practiced aloud until the order is clearly fixed in your mind and the wording is fluent. As you practice out loud, you will discover that, although the sequence of ideas is always the same, the choice of words varies somewhat each time you give it. And the words will not be exactly the same at the moment of actual presentation either. Spontaneity and flexibility are the two great advantages of this form of delivery.

In spite of its obvious advantages, you may decide against extemporaneous delivery for ceremonial speeches, however. The reason is that style—the choice of words—is of utmost importance in this type of address. Hence, the one element that is left somewhat unprepared in extemporaneous delivery is the one element that most distinguishes the outstanding from the mediocre ceremonial speech.

If your command of language is great enough, you may want to choose to speak extemporaneously; if you prefer not to leave the wording to chance, you may select either of the other two approaches.

[4] John F. Kennedy, "Ich Bin Ein Berliner," **The Burden and the Glory** (New York: Harper & Row, 1964), 98–99.

Memoriter delivery. You may decide to write out the address, commit it to memory, and give it without manuscript or notes. Memorizing the speech has some points in its favor: You can choose your language carefully and polish the style. If you do not have difficulty in memorizing or trouble in forgetting, you could achieve direct communication with your audience impossible when dependent on either notes or manuscript. On the other hand, there are some disadvantages: Many speakers recite badly, and the speech may **sound** memorized. Too, there is always the danger of awkward lapses while you search your memory for the pre-selected word or phrase. Have you ever seen that terror-struck look of panic cross a speaker's face when he, bereft of notes, manuscript, or friend to prompt, suddenly realized he did not know what came next? If so, that experience may have been enough to convince you to choose another form of delivery!

Manuscript delivery. The most common form of delivery at ceremonial occasions is reading from manuscript. There are several reasons: Writing the speech permits careful attention to choice and beauty of language. There is no excuse for incorrect grammar or imprecise wording. During the period you are composing the speech, you can consult books on usage, dictionaries, and a thesaurus. Writing the manuscript and reading it should insure polished style. In addition, using a manuscript allows you to time your address rather precisely. Since the speech must often fit into a rather rigid schedule for the program, exactness in timing is an important consideration. Finally, such speeches must sometimes be printed in advance for distribution immediately after the ceremony or they must be distributed to the press long before the actual presentation; prior publication may require a manuscript.

The disadvantages, of course, are rather obvious: Some speakers do not read well, losing the necessary lively sense of communication and directness. You must become so familiar with your manuscript that you can look directly at your audience often, glancing at your text to get a phrase and then looking at your listeners as you give it. You must also work to prevent a monotonous intonation pattern; your reading should have the same variety and vitality as your extemporaneous speaking.

Your task in reading is to communicate the intellectual and emotional meaning of the speech to the audience. Through your use of voice, the ideas and mood of the words you have committed to paper must come alive for your hearers. To achieve this purpose, you must give attention to three aspects of reading aloud: phrasing, pausing, and emphasizing.

Phrasing. We do not talk a word at a time; we should not read a word at a time. Instead, we speak in thought groups, units made up of a succession of words that logically hang together. The basic unit of oral communication is the phrase. The phrase may be only one word, such as "Never!" Or it may consist of a number of words, such as "There are no simple answers." The test is whether the group of words is a single idea.

When we are wording our thoughts as we think them, in conversation, and when we are reading thoughts we have preworded, in manuscript speaking, we must arrange our words into phrases if we are to make our meaning clear to our hearers. We do this grouping rather automatically in conversation, but we must work at it in reading. You must run your eyes along the succession of words on the printed page, sort them into sense groups, and give each phrase as a distinct unit to your listeners. Reading, then is a matter of looking, grouping, and saying. You should develop your eye span so you can get an entire phrase at a glance. This facility takes practice, but it can be developed.

Someone has said that proper phrasing is simple, just a matter of starting where you should and stopping where you should! I grant that this principle is the touchstone of phrasing, but I deny that it is simple. Many are misled by punctuation, which, though it may offer some clues, offers no infallible guides. You do not always pause at a comma, for example, and you may often stop the phrase where there is no punctuation at all. Look at this long sentence from a speech by Adlai Stevenson on United Nations Day in 1963, and decide where you would break it into phrases:

> On this United Nations Day, therefore, let us renew our hope that, finally, men will learn to live as brothers, to respect each other's differences, heal each other's wounds; promote each other's progress, and benefit from each other's knowledge.

Did you divide the sentence into eight thought groups? Although there is no one right way to phrase, I made the divisions as follows:

> On this United Nations Day therefore | let us renew our hope | that finally | men will learn to live as brothers | to respect each other's differences | heal each other's wounds | promote each other's progress | and benefit from each other's knowledge.

Pausing. Pauses are momentary silences, and their use is essential to communication of meaning and mood. For the speaker, the brief break in speaking provides an opportunity to look ahead at the next thought group, to think of a connective word or phrase that will make the relationships easier to convey, and to get a needed breath. For the listener, the short stop in the speaking gives an opportunity to digest what has been said or to get some added insight into importance and relationship of ideas.

Pauses occur between phrases. We have already discussed grouping of words into thought units; pausing is necessary after each phrase to indicate the end of the sense group. Pauses are our method of separating phrases from each other. It should be clear, then, that all pauses will not be the same length, but should be varied in terms of the relationship to be established. The pause at the end of a complete sentence will be longer than that between phrases within the sentence.

You will also use pauses within phrases, usually either before or after important words. If you use an anticipatory pause just before an unusually expressive or significant idea, you build up suspense and give the listeners a signal that what is coming packs a wallop. If you pause for an instant after a word expressing a major idea, you will heighten the dramatic effect and allow the audience to absorb it.

If your pauses are not mechanical waits or empty hesitations, but rather meaningful silences and if they are used to convey and reinforce ideas rather than just to catch your breath, they will be an important part of your communication when reading. Without adequate, well-timed pauses, your speech will sound rattled off. Pausing, as most small children could tell you, is an important technique in impressing.

Emphasizing. Focusing attention on words by means of higher pitch, longer duration, and increased volume is called emphasis. By stressing a word, we make it stand out in a phrase; we call attention to the fact that it is important; we give it prominence.

We use essentially the same techniques to emphasize a word as we use when stressing a syllable within a word. Pronounce the word **agreeable** aloud. Notice that the second syllable, the stressed syllable, is uttered on a higher frequency (pitch) than the other syllables, is held out longer than the other syllables, and is spoken more loudly than the others. Now say aloud the sentence, "I will **not** go!" and put the emphasis on the third word. You will see that **not** has higher pitch, longer duration, and greater force than the other words. Its implied meaning has been made absolutely explicit; the negative idea inherent in the word has been underscored by your use of voice.

To emphasize every word is to emphasize nothing. You must choose the words in each phrase that are to receive prominence and center attention on them. Generally, you should move to the thought-bearing words, the words that carry the main ideas, and let the less essential words fall into the background. Words that are necessary for our grammar but do not carry the principal ideas (such as articles, prepositions, conjunctions, auxiliary verbs, linking verbs, and relative pronouns) should be given less attention by weakening the vowels in them.

In addition to the thought-carrying words, you will also emphasize important new ideas, any word whose meaning you want to make explicit and definite (including articles, prepositions, etc.), and comparisons and contrasts.

In addition to phrasing, pausing, and emphasis, there are other important aspects of effective reading. Your reading, like every other method of delivery, should be as conversational as possible; it should sound natural. You must have a real sense of the meaning and mood at the moment of utterance; mechanically mouthing words will not communicate ideas and feelings. You should vary rate, melody, and quality of your voice to color in shades of meaning, intensify ideas, and vitalize concepts. The rate should vary with importance and purpose; the intonation pattern should be varied according to meaning (do not fall into a repetitious melody of sing-song, whine, or chant); and timbre should be appropriate for the emotion to be expressed. Delivering a speech from manuscript is not easy, but you **can** learn to read well and, with practice, can communicate directly and effectively with an audience from a prepared text.

Specimen eulogy

On November 7, 1962, Eleanor Roosevelt died. The newspapers quoted tributes from men in public life, but none made such an impression as the brief statement of Adlai Stevenson which included the sentence, "She would rather light candles than curse the darkness." He repeated the sentence a day later in his eulogy delivered at the United Nations.

The largest memorial service for Mrs. Roosevelt was held at the Cathedral Church of St. John the Divine on November 17, 1962. The next day the **New York Times** reported:

Ten thousand persons, including American and foreign diplomats, filled the Cathedral Church of St. John the Divine yesterday at a memorial service for Mrs. Franklin D. Roosevelt. . . . The Protestant Episcopal cathedral was crowded with young and old of all races and from all walks of life—women in furs and others in inexpensive cloth coats, whites, Negroes, and Asians. Every seat was occupied. Scores stood in the rear and in the aisles.[5]

Ambassador Adlai Stevenson, a close personal friend of Mrs. Roosevelt, delivered the principal address. According to the **Times,** "The audience sat hushed as Mr. Stevenson began his address. . . . Mr. Stevenson spoke from the pulpit, quietly but with obvious deep emotion. He wore a scarlet academic robe."[6]

The memorial service was a great outpouring of deeply felt grief and love. Mr. Stevenson obviously spoke for his hearers as well as to them.

In a eulogy that moved many in the audience to tears, Adlai Stevenson, United States representative to the United Nations, cited Mrs. Roosevelt for her efforts in behalf of the downtrodden and for world peace.[7]

The text of the address has been supplied by the Eleanor Roosevelt Memorial Foundation and is used with the permission of Adlai E. Stevenson III.

One week ago, in the rose garden at Hyde Park, Eleanor Roosevelt came home for the last time. Her journeys are over. The remembrance now begins.

In gathering here to honor her, we engage in a self-serving act. It is we who are trying, by this ceremony of tribute, to deny the fact that we have lost her, and, at least, to prolong the farewell, and—possibly—to say some of the things we dared not say in her presence, because she would have turned aside such testimonial with impatience and gently asked us to get on with some of the more serious business of the meeting.

A grief perhaps not equaled since the death of her husband seventeen years ago is the world's best tribute to one of the great figures of our age—a woman whose lucid and luminous faith testified always for sanity in an insane time and for hope in a time of obscure hope—a woman who spoke for the good toward which man aspires in a world which has seen too much of the evil of which man is capable.

She lived 78 years, most of the time in tireless activity as if she knew that

---

[5] "10,000 Attend Memorial Service for Mrs. Roosevelt," **The New York Times,** November 18, 1962, p. 71.
[6] Ibid.
[7] Ibid.

only a frail fragment of the things that cry out to be done could be done in the lifetime of even the most fortunate.

One has the melancholy sense that when she knew death was at hand, she was contemplating not what she achieved, but what she had not quite managed to do. And I know she wanted to go—when there was no more strength to do.

Yet how much she had done—how much still unchronicled! We dare not try to tabulate the lives she salvaged, the battles—known and unrecorded—she fought, the afflicted she comforted, the hovels she brightened, the faces and places, near and far, that were given some new radiance, some sound of music, by her endeavors. What other single human being has touched and transformed the existence of so many others? What better measure is there of the impact of anyone's life?

There was no sick soul too wounded to engage her mercy. There was no signal of human distress which she did not view as a personal summons. There was no affront to human dignity from which she fled because the timid cried "danger." And the number of occasions on which her intervention turned despair into victory we may never know.

Her life was crowded, restless, fearless. Perhaps she pitied most not those whom she aided in the struggle, but the more fortunate who were preoccupied with themselves and cursed with the self-deceptions of private success.

She walked in the slums and ghettos of the world, not on a tour of inspection, nor as a condescending patron, but as one who could not feel complacent while others were hungry, and who could not find contentment while others were in distress. This was not sacrifice; this, for Mrs. Roosevelt, was the only meaningful way of life.

These were not conventional missions of mercy. What rendered this unforgettable woman so extraordinary was not merely her response to suffering; it was her comprehension of the complexity of the human condition. Not long before she died, she wrote that "within all of us there are two sides. One reaches for the stars, the other descends to the level of beasts."

It was, I think, this discernment that made her so unfailingly tolerant of friends who faltered, and led her so often to remind the smug and the complacent that "There but for the grace of God . . ."

But we dare not regard her as just a benign incarnation of good works. For she was not only a great woman and a great humanitarian, but a great democrat. I use the word with a small "d"—though it was, of course, equally true that she was a great Democrat with a capital "D." When I say that she was a great small-d democrat, I mean that she had a lively and astute understanding of the nature of the democratic process. She was a master political strategist with a fine sense of humor. And, as she said, she loved a good fight.

She was a realist. Her compassion did not become sentimentality. She understood that progress was a long labor of compromise. She mistrusted absolutism in all its forms—the absolutism of the word and even more the absolutism of the deed. She never supposed that all the problems of life could be cured in a day or a year or a lifetime. Her pungent and salty understanding of human behavior kept her always in intimate contact with reality. I think this was a primary source of her strength, because she never thought that the loss of a battle meant the loss of a war, nor did she suppose that a compromise which produced only part of the objective sought was an act of corruption or of treachery. She knew that no formula of words, no combination of deeds, could abolish the troubles of life overnight and usher in the millennium.

The miracle, I have tried to suggest, is how much tangible good she really did; how much realism and reason were mingled with her instinctive compassion; how her contempt for the perquisites of power ultimately won her the esteem of so many of the powerful; and how, at her death, there was a universality of grief that transcended all the harsh boundaries of political, racial, and religious strife and, for a moment at least, united men in a vision of what their world might be.

We do not claim the right to enshrine another mortal, and this least of all would Mrs. Roosevelt have desired. She would have wanted it said, I believe, that she well knew the pressures of pride and vanity, the sting of bitterness and defeat, the gray days of national peril and personal anguish. But she clung to the confident expectation that men could fashion their own tomorrows if they could only learn that yesterday can be neither relived nor revised.

Many who have spoken of her in these last few days have used a word to which we all assent, because it speaks a part of what we feel. They have called her "a lady," a "great lady," "the first lady of the world." But the word "lady," though it says much about Eleanor Roosevelt, does not say all. To be incapable of self-concern is not a negative virtue; it is the other side of a coin that has a positive face—the most positive, I think, of all the faces. And to enhance the humanity of others is not a kind of humility; it is a kind of pride—the noblest of all the forms of pride. No man or woman can respect other men and women who does not respect life. And to respect life is to love it. Eleanor Roosevelt loved life—and that, perhaps, is the most meaningful thing that can be said about her, for it says so much beside.

It takes courage to love life. Loving it demands imagination and perception and the kind of patience women are more apt to have than men—the bravest and most understanding women. And loving it takes something more besides—it takes a gift for life, a gift for love.

Eleanor Roosevelt's childhood was unhappy—miserably unhappy, she sometimes said. But it was Eleanor Roosevelt who also said that "one must

never, for whatever reason, turn his back on life." She did not mean that
duty should compel us. She meant that life should. "Life," she said, "was
meant to be lived." A simple statement. An obvious statement. But a statement that by its obviousness and its simplicity challenges the most intricate
of all the philosophies of despair.

Many of the admonitions she bequeathed us are neither new thoughts nor
novel concepts. Her ideas were, in many respects, old-fashioned—as old as
the Sermon on the Mount, as the reminder that it is more blessed to give
than to receive, in the words of St. Francis that she loved so well: "For it is
in the giving that we receive."

She imparted to the familiar language—nay, what too many have come to
treat as the clichés—of Christianity a new poignancy and vibrance. She did
so not by reciting them, but by proving that it is possible to live them.

It is this above all that rendered her unique in her century. It was said of
her contemptuously at times that she was a do-gooder, a charge leveled with
similar derision against another public figure born 1,962 years ago.

We who are assembled here are of various religious and political faiths,
and perhaps different conceptions of man's destiny in the universe. It is not
an irreverence, I trust, to say that the immortality Mrs. Roosevelt would
have valued most would be found in the deeds and visions her life inspired
in others, and in the proof that they would be faithful to the spirit of any
tribute conducted in her name.

And now one can almost hear Mrs. Roosevelt saying that the speaker has
already talked too long. So we must say farewell. We are always saying
farewell in this world—always standing at the edge of loss attempting to
retrieve some memory, some human meaning, from the silence—something
which was precious and is gone.

Often, although we know the absence well enough, we cannot name it or
describe it even. What left the world when Lincoln died? Speaker after
speaker in those aching days tried to tell his family or his neighbors or his
congregation. But no one found the words, not even Whitman. "When lilacs
last in the dooryard bloomed" can break the heart, but not with Lincoln's
greatness, only with his loss. What the words could never capture was the
man himself. His deeds were known; every school child knew them. But it
was not his deeds the country mourned, it was the man—the mastery of life
which made the greatness of the man.

It is always so. On that April day when Franklin Roosevelt died, it was not
a President we wept for. It was a man. In Archibald MacLeish's words:

> Fagged out, worn down, sick
> With the weight of his own bones, the
>   task finished,
> The war won, the victory assured,
> The glory left behind him for the
>   others,

And the wheels roll up through the
        night in the sweet land
In the cool air in the spring between
        the lanterns.

It is so now. What we have lost in Eleanor Roosevelt is not her life. She lived that out to the full. What we have lost, what we wish to recall for ourselves, to remember, is what she was herself. And who can name it? But she left "a name to shine on the entablatures of truth, forever."

We pray that she has found peace, and a glimpse of sunset. But today we weep for ourselves. We are lonelier; someone has gone from one's own life —who was like the certainty of refuge; and someone has gone from the world—who was like a certainty of honor.

Questions for specimen speech analysis

1. Was Mr. Stevenson able to compose a tribute without relying on the trite? Is the speech moving without seeming maudlin? Why or why not?

2. Did the speaker pay tribute in terms of the ideals, values, aspirations, and traditions of the hearers? Cite specific instances to support your answer. What sentiments did Mr. Stevenson presuppose?

3. What specific events from the life of Mrs. Roosevelt provided material for this speech? How effectively were these materials used?

4. Is it clear from the address that Mr. Stevenson and Mrs. Roosevelt were close friends? Were there any personal references? If so, were they tastefully handled?

5. Did Mr. Stevenson utilize allusions, comparisons, contrasts, examples, factual information, illustrations, anecdotes, or quotations for supporting material? If so, how did he integrate them into the address? Were they particularly appropriate, and if so, why?

6. Was the address well organized? Was the brief introduction appropriate for the subject, audience, and occasion? Why? Was the transition into the conclusion similar to the one between the introduction and body? Were those references to Mrs. Roosevelt fitting transitions? Why? Did the progressions of thought move smoothly without awkward jumps? Was the conclusion an impressive climax for the address?

7. Was the language of the speech "esthetically pleasing?" Were the ideas presented in a meaningful and memorable way? Were the words clear, appropriate, and vivid? Were the sentences varied in type and form? Were the sentences clear and straightforward? Did Mr. Stevenson avoid clichés?

8. Did the speaker use rhetorical devices to enhance the dignity and effectiveness of the address? Did Mr. Stevenson use metaphors effectively?

Did he utilize parallelism and antithesis? Cite specific examples. Did the use of stylistic devices contribute to his purpose?

9. Did Mr. Stevenson manage to avoid the extremes of flippancy and over-sentimentality? Did the speech give the impression of emotion deeply, sincerely felt? Did you find the address moving?

Specimen speech for commencement

The Association of Graduates of the United States Military Academy annually presents the Sylvanus Thayer Medal to a citizen whose service to the United States exemplifies the ideals of the military academy's motto: "Duty, Honor, Country."

On May 12, 1962, General Douglas MacArthur, then 82, went to West Point, for the last time, to accept the award. General MacArthur was noted for his eloquence; all his public utterances were polished and revealed concern for and attention to style. In this address, delivered without manuscript or notes, he displayed again his characteristic elegance of language.

Although this speech is not a commencement address, it offers an excellent example of an inspirational speech suitable for such an occasion. Addressed to the cadets of the academy, with which he had strong personal ties (not only was he a graduate, he had served at one time as superintendent of the academy), the speech was a touching tribute to the Long Grey Line and a moving challenge to honor its traditional ideals.

As I was leaving the hotel this morning, a doorman asked me "Where are you bound for, General?" And when I replied, "West Point," he remarked, "Beautiful place. Have you ever been there before?"

No human being could ever fail to be deeply moved by such a tribute as this, coming from a profession I have served so long and a people I have loved so well. It fills me with an emotion I cannot express. But this award is not intended primarily to honor a personality, but to symbolize a great moral code—the code of conduct, of chivalry, of those who guard this beloved land of culture and ancient descent. That is the animation of this medallion. For all eyes and for all time it is an expression of the ethics of the American soldier. That I should be integrated in this way with so noble an ideal arouses a sense of pride, and yet of humility, which will be with me always.

Duty. Honor. Country. Those three hallowed words reverently dictate what you want to be, what you can be, what you will be. They are your rallying point to build courage when courage seems to fail, to regain faith when there seems to be little cause for faith, to create hope when hope becomes forlorn. Unhappily, I possess neither that eloquence of dictation, that poetry of imagination, nor that brilliance of metaphor, to tell you all that they mean. The unbelievers will say they are but words, but a slogan, but a flamboyant phrase. Every pedant, every demagogue, every cynic, every hypocrite, every troublemaker, and, I am sorry to say, some others of an entirely different nature, will try to downgrade them even to the extent of mockery and ridicule.

But these are some of the things they do. They build your basic character. They mold you for your future roles as the custodians of the nation's defense. They make you strong enough to know when you are weak and brave enough to face yourself when you are afraid. They teach you to be proud and unbending in honest failure, but humble and gentle in success; not to substitute words for actions; not to seek the path of comfort, but to face the stress and spur of difficulty and challenge; to learn to stand up in the storm, but to have compassion on those who fall; to master yourself before you seek to master others; to have a heart that is clean, a goal that is high; to learn to laugh, yet never forget how to weep; to reach into the future, yet never neglect the past; to be serious, yet never take yourself too seriously; to be modest so that you will remember the simplicity of true greatness, the open mind of true wisdom, the meekness of true strength. They give you a temper of the will, a vigor of the emotions, a freshness of the deep springs of life, a temperamental predominance of courage over timidity, of an appetite for adventure over love of ease. They create in your heart the sense of wonder, the unfailing hope of what next, and the joy and inspiration of life. They teach you in this way to be an officer and a gentleman.

And what sort of soldiers are those you are to lead? Are they reliable? Are they brave? Are they capable of victory? Their story is known to all of you. It is the story of the American man-at-arms. My estimate of him was formed on the battlefields many, many years ago, and has never changed. I regarded him then, as I regard him now, as one of the world's noblest figures— not only as one of the finest military characters, but also as one of the most stainless. His name and fame are the birthright of every American citizen. In his youth and strength, his love and loyalty, he gave all that mortality can give.

He needs no eulogy from me or any other man. He has written his own history, and written it in red on his enemy's breast. But when I think of his patience under adversity, of his courage under fire, and his modesty in victory, I am filled with an emotion of admiration I cannot put into words. He belongs to history as furnishing one of the greatest examples of successful patriotism; he belongs to posterity as the instructor of future generations in the principles of liberty and freedom; he belongs to the present, to us, by his virtues and by his achievements.

In twenty campaigns, on a hundred battlefields, around a thousand campfires I have witnessed that enduring fortitude, that patriotic self-abnegation, and that invincible determination which has carved his statue in the hearts of his people. From one end of the world to the other he has drained deep the chalice of courage.

As I listened to those songs, in memory's eye I could see those staggering columns of the First World War, bending under soggy packs on many a weary march from dripping dusk to drizzling dawn; slogging ankle-deep through the mire of shell-pocked roads to form grimly for the attack, blue-lipped, covered with sludge and mud, chilled by the wind and rain; driving home to their objective, and, for many, to the judgment seat of God. I do not know the dignity of their birth. But I do know the glory of their death. They died unquestioning, uncomplaining, with faith in their hearts, and on their lips the hope that we would go on to victory. Always for them: duty, honor, country. Always their blood, and sweat, and tears, as we saw the way, and the light, and the truth.

And 20 years after, on the other side of the globe, again the filth of dirty foxholes, the stench of ghostly trenches, the slime of dripping dugouts, those boiling suns of relentless heat, those torrential rains of devastating storms, the loneliness and utter desolation of jungle trails, the bitterness of long separation from those they loved and cherished, the deadly pestilence of tropical disease, the horror of stricken areas of the war. Their resolute and determined defense, their swift and sure attack, their indomitable purpose, their complete and decisive victory—always victory. Always through the bloody haze of their last reverberating shot, the vision of gaunt, ghastly men, reverently following your password of duty, honor, country.

The code which those words perpetuate embraces the highest moral law and will stand the test of any ethics or philosophies ever promulgated for the uplift of mankind. Its requirements are for the things that are right and its restraints are from the things that are wrong. The soldier, above all other men, is required to practice the greatest act of religious training—sacrifice. In battle and in the face of danger and death he discloses those divine attributes which his Maker gave when he created man in his own image. No physical courage and no brute instinct can take the place of the divine help, which alone can sustain him. However horrible the incidents of war may be, the soldier who is called upon to offer and to give his life for his country is the noblest development of mankind.

You now face a new world, a world of change. The thrust into outer space of the satellite spheres and missiles marks a beginning of another epoch in the long story of mankind. In the five-or-more billions of years the scientists tell us it has taken to form the earth, in the three-or-more billions of years of development of the human race, there has never been a more abrupt or staggering evolution.

We deal now, not with things of this world alone, but with the illimitable distances and as yet unfathomed mysteries of the universe. We are reaching out for a new and boundless frontier. We speak in strange terms of harnessing the cosmic energy, of making winds and tides work for us, of creating synthetic materials to supplement or even replace our old standard basics, to purify sea water for our drink, of preventatives to expand life into hundreds of years, of controlling the weather for a more equitable distribution of heat and cold, of rain and shine, of space ships to the moon, of the primary target in war no longer limited to the armed forces of an enemy, but instead to include his civil populations, of ultimate conflicts between a united human race and a sinister force of some other planetary galaxy, of such dreams and fantasies as to make life the most exciting of all times.

And through all this welter of change and development your mission remains fixed, determined, inviolable. It is to win our wars. Everything else in your professional career is but corollary to this vital dedication. All other public purposes, all other public projects, all other public needs, great or small, will find others for their accomplishments; but you are the ones trained to fight. Yours is the profession of arms: the will to win, the sure knowledge that in war there is no substitute for victory, that if you lose the nation will be destroyed, that the very obsession of your public service must be duty, honor, country.

Others will debate the controversial issues, national and international, which divide men's minds. But serene, calm, aloof, you stand as the nation's war guardians, as its lifeguards from the raging tides of international conflicts, as its gladiators in the arena of battle. For a century-and-a-half you have defended, guarded, and protected its hallowed traditions of liberty and freedom, of right and justice.

Let civilian voices argue the merits or demerits of our processes of government: whether our strength is being sapped by deficit financing indulged in too long, by federal paternalism grown too mighty, by power groups grown too arrogant, by politics grown too corrupt, by crime grown rampant, by morals grown too low, by taxes grown too high, by extremists grown too violent; whether our personal liberties are as firm and complete as they should be. These great national problems are not for your professional participation or military solution. Your guidepost stands out like a tenfold beacon in the night: duty, honor, country.

You are the lever which binds together the entire fabric of our national system of defense. From your ranks come the great captains who hold the nation's destiny in their hands the moment the war tocsin sounds. The long gray line has never failed us. Were you to do so, a million ghosts in olive drab, in brown khaki, in blue and gray, would rise from their white crosses, thundering those magic words: duty, honor, country.

This does not mean that you are warmongers. On the contrary, the soldier above all other people prays for peace, for he must suffer and bear the deepest wounds and scars of war. But always in our ears ring the ominous words of Plato, that wisest of all philosophers, "Only the dead have seen the end of war."

The shadows are lengthening for me. The twilight is here. My days of old have vanished—tone and tints. They have gone glimmering through the things that were. Their memory is one of wondrous beauty watered by tears and coaxed and caressed by the smiles of yesterday.

I listen vainly, but with thirsty ear, for the witching melody of faint bugles blowing reveille, of far drums beating the long roll. In my dreams I hear again the crash of guns, the rattle of musketry, the strange, mournful mutter of the battlefield. But in the evening of my memory, always I come back to West Point. Always there echoes and re-echoes: duty, honor, country.

Today marks my final roll call with you. But I want you to know that when I cross the river, my last conscious thoughts will be of The Corps, and The Corps, and The Corps. I bid you farewell.

Questions for specimen speech analysis

1. Did General MacArthur have one central theme for his message? Was everything in the speech clearly related to that theme? Were there any tangents or digressions? If so, did they detract from the address?

2. Was the theme appropriate for the speaker, audience, and occasion?

3. Did General MacArthur utilize the values, ideals, aspirations, and traditions of his listeners as materials for his address? Did he utilize them effectively? Cite specific instances and evaluate them.

4. Did General MacArthur use allusions, comparisons, contrasts, examples, illustrations, anecdotes, facts, or quotations? Cite specific instances and evaluate their use as supporting material.

5. What kinds of reasoning did General MacArthur employ? Were his arguments sound?

6. To what emotions did General MacArthur appeal? Were those appeals tastefully handled? Could General MacArthur reminisce without seeming maudlin?

7. How did the speaker establish common ground with his audience in the introduction? How did he seek to increase his personal credibility, his **ethos?** How did he acknowledge the occasion and move into his theme?

8. Was the speech clearly, coherently structured? Were there balanced divisions? Were there smooth transitions to relate the parts to each other? Is the progression of thought easy to follow? Was the conclusion fitting, impressive, memorable, moving?

9. Was the language of the speech "esthetically pleasing?" Was it lofty,

forceful, and imaginative? Was it in places ostentatious, wordy, or euphuistic?

10. What metaphors did General MacArthur employ? Were they fresh, vivid, and arresting? Did he sometimes use mixed metaphors? Was the imagery ever overdone? Did he employ clichés?

11. Did the use of such stylistic devices as parallelism, refrain, and rhetorical questions contribute to the effectiveness of his style and to his purpose of inspiration? Cite specific instances.

Specimen inaugural address

As thousands descended on Washington for the inauguration of the thirty-fifth President of the United States, a blizzard hit the East Coast and deposited eight inches of snow on the capital city. Three thousand servicemen worked through the night before the inauguration to clear the streets for the inaugural parade, and the ceremony was held as scheduled.

The sun shone, but the temperature was twenty-two degrees, and the thousands present shivered through the ceremony. The new President, the youngest man ever elected to that office, removed his overcoat before advancing to the lectern to deliver his inaugural address. If he was cold or uncomfortable, he did not reveal it as he spoke.

The inauguration of the new President on January 20, 1961 was unique in many ways. Robert Frost read; Marian Anderson sang; and John F. Kennedy spoke. As Arthur M. Schlesinger, Jr., has written, "The Kennedy Presidency began with incomparable dash."[8]

The Inaugural Address was carefully prepared. Theodore Sorensen observed, "No Kennedy speech ever underwent so many drafts. Each paragraph was reworded, reworked, and reduced."[9] Many advisers offered suggestions for the speech, but according to Sorensen, "however numerous the assistant artisans, the principal architect of the Inaugural Address was John Fitzgerald Kennedy."[10] Kennedy placed great emphasis on the address, because, says Sorensen, "he wanted it to set a tone for the era about to begin."[11]

[8] Arthur M. Schlesinger, Jr., **A Thousand Days** (Boston: Houghton Mifflin Company, 1965), 165.
[9] Theodore C. Sorensen, **Kennedy** (New York: Harper & Row, 1965), 241.
[10] Ibid.
[11] Theodore C. Sorensen, **Kennedy** (New York: Harper & Row, 1965), 240. See pp. 240–245 for an interesting account of the preparation of this address.

Kennedy read from a large-type reading copy, and he spent as much time in advance as possible familiarizing himself with the text. The importance he attached to the address was evident in his delivery; he spoke slowly and deliberately in a clear, firm voice.

We observe today not a victory of party but a celebration of freedom, symbolizing an end as well as a beginning, signifying renewal as well as change. For I have sworn before you and Almighty God the same solemn oath our forebears prescribed nearly a century and three-quarters ago.

The world is very different now. For man holds in his mortal hands the power to abolish all forms of human poverty and all forms of human life. And yet the same revolutionary belief for which our forebears fought is still at issue around the globe, the belief that the rights of man come not from the generosity of the state but from the hand of God.

We dare not forget today that we are the heirs of that first revolution. Let the word go forth from this time and place, to friend and foe alike, that the torch has been passed to a new generation of Americans, born in this century, tempered by war, disciplined by a hard and bitter peace, proud of our ancient heritage, and unwilling to witness or permit the slow undoing of those human rights to which this nation has always been committed, and to which we are committed today at home and around the world.

Let every nation know, whether it wishes us well or ill, that we shall pay any price, bear any burden, meet any hardship, support any friend, oppose any foe to assure the survival and the success of liberty.

This much we pledge—and more.

To those old allies whose cultural and spiritual origins we share, we pledge the loyalty of faithful friends. United, there is little we cannot do in a host of cooperative ventures. Divided, there is little we can do, for we dare not meet a powerful challenge at odds and split asunder.

To those new states whom we welcome to the ranks of the free, we pledge our word that one form of colonial control shall not have passed away merely to be replaced by a far more iron tyranny. We shall not always expect to find them supporting our view. But we shall always hope to find them strongly supporting their own freedom, and to remember that, in the past, those who foolishly sought power by riding the back of the tiger ended up inside.

To those peoples in the huts and villages of half the globe struggling to break the bonds of mass misery, we pledge our best efforts to help them help themselves, for whatever period is required, not because the Communists may be doing it, not because we seek their votes, but because it is right. If a free society cannot help the many who are poor, it cannot save the few who are rich.

To our sister republics south of our border, we offer a special pledge: to convert our good words into good deeds, in a new alliance for progress, to assist free men and free governments in casting off the chains of poverty. But this peaceful revolution of hope cannot become the prey of hostile powers. Let all our neighbors know that we shall join with them to oppose aggression or subversion anywhere in the Americas. And let every other power know that this hemisphere intends to remain the master of its own house.

To that world assembly of sovereign states, the United Nations, our last best hope in an age where the instruments of war have far outpaced the instruments of peace, we renew our pledge of support: to prevent it from becoming merely a forum for invective, to strengthen its shield of the new and the weak, and to enlarge the area in which its writ may run.

Finally, to those nations who would make themselves our adversary, we offer not a pledge but a request: that both sides begin anew the quest for peace, before the dark powers of destruction unleashed by science engulf all humanity in planned or accidental self-destruction.

We dare not tempt them with weakness. For only when our arms are sufficient beyond doubt can we be certain beyond doubt that they will never be employed.

But neither can two great and powerful groups of nations take comfort from our present course—both sides overburdened by the cost of modern weapons, both rightly alarmed by the steady spread of the deadly atom, yet both racing to alter that uncertain balance of terror that stays the hand of mankind's final war.

So let us begin anew, remembering on both sides that civility is not a sign of weakness, and sincerity is always subject to proof. Let us never negotiate out of fear, but let us never fear to negotiate.

Let both sides explore what problems unite us instead of belaboring those problems which divide us.

Let both sides, for the first time, formulate serious and precise proposals for the inspection and control of arms, and bring the absolute power to destroy other nations under the absolute control of all nations.

Let both sides seek to invoke the wonders of science instead of its terrors. Together let us explore the stars, conquer the deserts, eradicate disease, tap the ocean depths and encourage the arts and commerce.

Let both sides unite to heed in all corners of the earth the command of Isaiah to "undo the heavy burdens . . . [and] let the oppressed go free."

And if a beachhead of cooperation may push back the jungle of suspicion, let both sides join in creating a new endeavor, not a new balance of power, but a new world of law, where the strong are just and the weak secure and the peace preserved.

All this will not be finished in the first one hundred days. Nor will it be finished in the first one thousand days, nor in the life of this Administration, nor even perhaps in our lifetime on this planet. But let us begin.

In your hands, my fellow citizens, more than mine, will rest the final success or failure of our course. Since this country was founded, each generation of Americans has been summoned to give testimony to its national loyalty. The graves of young Americans who answered the call to service surround the globe.

Now the trumpet summons us again—not as a call to bear arms, though arms we need; not as a call to battle, though embattled we are; but a call to bear the burden of a long twilight struggle, year in and year out, "rejoicing in hope, patient in tribulation," a struggle against the common enemies of man: tyranny, poverty, disease and war itself.

Can we forge against these enemies a grand and global alliance, North and South, East and West, that can assure a more fruitful life for all mankind? Will you join in that historic effort?

In the long history of the world, only a few generations have been granted the role of defending freedom in its hour of maximum danger. I do not shrink from this responsibility; I welcome it. I do not believe that any of us would exchange places with any other people or any other generation. The energy, the faith, the devotion which we bring to this endeavor will light our country and all who serve it, and the glow from that fire can truly light the world.

And so, my fellow Americans, ask not what your country can do for you; ask what you can do for your country.

My fellow citizens of the world, ask not what America will do for you, but what together we can do for the freedom of man.

Finally, whether you are citizens of America or citizens of the world, ask of us here the same high standards of strength and sacrifice we ask of you. With a good conscience our only sure reward, with history the final judge of our deeds, let us go forth to lead the land we love, asking His blessing and His help, but knowing that here on earth God's work must truly be our own.

Questions for specimen speech analysis

1. Did President Kennedy's address have a central theme? Were there digressions?

2. Was the theme appropriate for the speaker, audience, and occasion?

3. What supporting materials did President Kennedy employ? Did he use American values, ideals, aspirations, and traditions? Cite specific instances. Did he utilize them effectively? Did he utilize allusions, comparisons, contrasts, examples, illustrations, anecdotes, facts, or quotations? Cite specific instances and evaluate their use.

4. What kinds of reasoning did President Kennedy employ? Was it sound?

5. To what emotions did he appeal? How were those appeals handled?

6. How did President Kennedy seek to strengthen his own "image" through his words?

7. How was the address structured? Were there clear, logically discreet divisions? Were there transitions to make relationships clear? Was the progression of thought easy to follow? Were the introduction and conclusion fitting?

8. Was the language of the address "esthetically pleasing?" Was it lofty, forceful, imaginative? Was it vivid, clear, impressive, memorable?

9. What imagery, if any, did President Kennedy employ? What stylistic devices did he use? How would you evaluate them? What is the most distinctive element of his style?

10. Did the wording of the speech contribute to the purpose (inspiration)? How? Why? Be specific.

Keynote or rally speeches

Purpose

The inspirational speaker at a rally or the keynote speaker at a convention faces a difficult task. Through his words, he must lift spirits, heighten expectations, deepen commitment, and generate zeal.

When the West Point football captain speaks to the assembled cadets at the rally preceding the game with Navy, he does not aim primarily at informing his listeners about football techniques nor instructing them in team strategy. Nor does he try to persuade them to prefer his team to the opposition! His hearers are somewhat partisan already, and his goal is simply to stir them to more intense fervor, to more enthusiastic support.

When the keynote speaker addresses his fellow delegates at a Republican or Democratic national convention, he does not attempt to inform the restive audience about American history or political theory; he does not waste time convincing the already convinced to vote for his party; he seeks rather to arouse the enthusiasm of the party faithful and to stimulate their latent devotion to the party's cause.

Like the clarion trumpeter of old, the rally speaker sounds the signal to unite and advance. The rally speech is, then, a call to arms, a war cry, and is primarily emotional in its appeal. The speaker's purpose is to inspire,[12] to incite, to motivate. He must take the ideals presumably held by the audience and make them vital; he must take beliefs he shares with his listeners and make them impelling; he must take nominal loyalties of his hearers and turn them into active commitments. If he is successful, he will stir his audience to renewed dedication and steadfast resolution.

Occasion

The term **rally** was originally a military term, but it has now taken on metaphoric meaning for other kinds of gatherings. An army, when it was scattered or disorganized, rallied, which is to say it reunited for renewed, concentrated effort. People who are ill are said to rally when they summon new strength and move toward recovery. Mass-meetings are called rallies in the United States, because through those meetings groups, organizations, or movements assemble to consolidate their forces, to revive their vigor, and to concentrate their energies.

Rallies are those meetings where the goal is unity of purpose and singleness of will. The organizers of the meeting want the audience to respond with active support; the audience comes to the meeting to be challenged and moved. Any group or any organization may at some time hold a rally, and rallies are characteristic of most mass movements. Wherever there is a "cause," there is the possibility of rallies; indeed, they are almost inevitable. Through meetings and speechmaking the forces are gathered.

Your school doubtless has rallies to enlist enthusiastic support for its organized sports programs. There are probably also many rallies for the various candidates during your campaigns for officers of your student government. And the Young Democrats and Young Republicans must rally their adherents during the state and national political campaigns!

Politics and public affairs afford many occasions to rally. Not only are there rallies held in connection with political conventions, there are also rallies of workers in every campaign for charity and public causes. The YMCA fund drive is always preceded by a rally (often held

---

[12] The word **inspire** is especially appropriate to describe the purpose of the rally speaker. The word **inspire** means, literally, "to breathe into," and the speaker does hope to breathe fire into the spirits of his listeners.

in connection with a dinner) of those who are responsible for raising the money; fund-raisers for the United Fund usually are gathered for encouragement and exhortation; church groups (especially youth organizations) hold countless rallies to revive and renew flagging devotion. Indeed, all civic, charitable, and religious organizations hold rallies.

And business is not exempt; it, too, sees the need for gathering people to motivate them. Sales promotion meetings, for example, are held regularly in many businesses to encourage company representatives to do their best. Some executives might resent having these meetings called "rallies," but they have the same purpose and the same kind of speechmaking is in order.

The distinctive aspect of the rally, from your point of view as speaker, is that the audience ordinarily has something in common that is quite basic to your purpose. You have a much more homogeneous audience than most speakers have. Although you may have to overcome indifference, you will not have the disadvantage of facing hostility. Your listeners are likely to grant your assumptions, because they share your loyalties and values. They come to hear you because they feel they belong; they are willing to be stirred and encouraged. You will have to interest them and touch them, but you will not have to persuade them first.

One other aspect of the rally occasion is in your favor when you speak, as well. The physical surroundings are often conducive to inspiration. If the arrangements committee has planned wisely and worked efficiently, the room or hall will be arranged and decorated to contribute to your purpose. If it is a political rally, there will be flags, bunting, and posters; if it is a religious rally held in a place of worship, the very architecture and the furnishings should establish an appropriate mood; if it is a sports rally, there may be a bonfire (the ancients knew the impressive influence of fire) and live players to help focus enthusiasm. If the place of meeting is especially fitting, use it to contribute to your goal of inspiration. If possible, let the setting work for you.

Preparation

Although the primary purpose of the rally speech is to inspire, not to inform or persuade, and although the speech will be primarily emotional rather than factual or logical in its construction and appeal, you should not be misled into thinking you need not prepare.

To touch the deep feelings of men, to move them (so that they stay moved) to active concern (which will remain after the speechmaking and the impressive pageantry of the moment are long past), you must analyze your audience thoroughly and plan your appeals carefully. Preparation is absolutely necessary.

Topics. The choice of topics for the rally speech is limited somewhat by the nature of the purpose, the occasion, the audience, and the group sponsoring the meeting. Your subject should be appropriate in view of all four considerations.

Ask yourself, therefore, why will these people be gathered? Around what are they being asked to unite? What is the cause they are being asked to support? Your topic should contribute to accomplishing the purpose of the meeting.

Ask yourself if the occasion, the time and place of meeting, require certain kinds of topics and eliminate others. Where will the meeting take place? What kind of atmosphere or mood will be established by the surroundings? Is the meeting part of the larger program or series of meetings, and if so how must it fit into the larger whole? Is the meeting the opening or culmination of a campaign? Is the gathering an organizational meeting? Will other speakers also address the group, and how will your role relate to theirs? Would your audience consider any topics or kind of treatment in poor taste in these particular circumstances or surroundings? Your subject must be appropriate for the occasion.

Then ask yourself what the audience will have in common. Will they all be members of the same political party, or of the same church, or of the same club? Will they all have a common interest in the movement to be supported? Are they all of the same nationality, or sex, or age? Are they all of the same cultural background, and do they all share the same system of values? Then, after you have considered the relevant elements of your audience, ask what subject would reach all these people for the cause you are called on to support. Your topic must be appropriate for the audience.

If you are going to address a rally, someone invited you to speak. Some person or some group has organized the mass meeting. There is a movement to be mobilized, forces to be united, an organization to be served. You must ask yourself what the sponsors expect and what topic would best enlist support for their cause. Your subject should be appropriate for the sponsoring organization.

Materials. A rally speech is a speech to stimulate, and the materials must be selected with that purpose in mind. The speech must be built out of those things that human beings get excited about. What are they? The basic drives or motivating forces common to almost all men, the sentiments or attitudes learned and adopted by individuals, and the emotions or feelings with which these people respond to the stimuli in their environment.

Fundamental drives. Schopenhauer's comment that human beings can do what they want, but cannot want what they want is profound and relevant. Human beings do not select their basic desires, wants, needs; those drives are built in. However you may deal with them, even if you repress the desires, the drives are there. You may will strongly enough not to yield to them, but you cannot will them out of existence.

Admittedly, psychologists are not agreed either on the universality of drives or on the list to be compiled. Many, however, would agree on the following four fundamental human motives:

1. Self-preservation.
2. Comfort and well-being.
3. Self-esteem.
4. Sex.

You may fight to protect yourself if you think your life is in danger; you may prefer a dormitory room with air conditioning if you must go to summer school; you may refuse to buy that "greasy kid stuff," since you want to be considered an adult; and you may do your part to preserve the human race from extinction. Surely all of us are aware of the power of these four fundamental drives in our own experience.

At times, of course, we are subjected to conflicting motives, and we must establish at that moment a priority system among them. There may be a conflict within you, for example, between your sex drive and your drive for self-esteem. Or there may be a conflict between your desire for self-respect and your need for self preservation. Have you ever been tempted to cheat or to commit other cowardly acts only to face the fact that you could not live with yourself if you did so? What you decide will depend on which drive for you is stronger at the moment!

If it is true that these four drives are basic to all of us, and if success in the rally speech involves setting these fundamental forces in
motion within the members of the audience, the logical question
is: how can that tas... be accomplished? How does the speaker "turn
on" these powerful devices? Generally, he does not approach
them directly, but indirectly through appeals to sentiments and
emotions.

Sentiments. Sentiments are composite mental attitudes derived from
the environment. They are learned, selected, adopted; they are the
result of cultural conditioning. We seem to absorb them from our
parents, our relatives, our friends, our associates. Oscar Hammer-
stein II stated the truth exceptionally well in **South Pacific:** "You Have
To Be Carefully Taught!"

Sentiments, then, are the values, loyalties, viewpoints, assumptions,
and beliefs which form the basis for decisions and behavior. If you
want to stir audiences, to move and arouse them, you must appeal to
the sentiments they already hold. You must identify the cause you
are expounding, the organization you are supporting, or the group you
are representing with positive attitudes of your listeners.

Appealing to beliefs they do not hold or to ideals they do not share
is futile and vain. You must analyze your audience in order to find
the suitable basis for appeals.

First, ask yourself what values they hold. What do they consider
worthy of respect? What do they consider unworthy? What do they
hold in awe, and what do they hold in contempt? To what do they
attach highest priorities, and what do they think unimportant and
trivial? What would they rate good or approvable? What would they
evaluate as poor, evil or unacceptable?

Next, ask yourself what loyalties your audience has. To what do they
claim to owe allegiance? Which loyalties are most important to them?
With what organizations, groups, or movements do they feel identified? Are there strong bonds with family, friends, church, club, fraternity, political party, school, city, state, region, or nation?

You should also ask yourself what viewpoints or biases your audience might have. What prejudices, what predilections, what leanings,
what frame of mind or "mind-set" will they have? Will they tend to
be conservative and opposed to most change? Are they predisposed in
favor of innovations? Are they likely to be close-minded and hostile
to new ideas? Do they usually react reflectively or reflexively?

Another approach to analyzing the values of the audience might be to ask yourself what assumptions they grant and what ones they reject. What are the premises on which they operate? What are the presuppositions which they do not examine, question, or doubt? What are the hypotheses that form the basis of their reasoning and their lives?

Finally, you might ask yourself what your audience believes or what it believes in. What tenets, principles, or doctrines will the audience all have in common? What opinions will they share? To what creeds will they subscribe? What precepts will they intend to follow? What convictions will they hold? To what will they give credence, and whom or what will they think credible? In whom or what do they have confidence and faith?

After analyzing the audience, to determine the sentiments it is likely to have in common, you must choose appeals to enlist those sentiments in support of your cause. If your audience values self-reliance, then you must show that what you support would produce self-reliant individuals. If your audience is loyal to the Moose lodge, you must show that support for your cause would strengthen the Moose chapter. If your audience is biased against change, then you must show that what you support will preserve our noblest and most cherished traditions. If your audience assumes that an intelligent Being created the universe, you would either assume the same thing or keep quiet on the subject. If your audience has confidence in the wisdom of Spiro Agnew, you could find a quotation in one of his speeches to indicate he is in favor of the same cause you are. Find those sentiments common to all or most of your hearers, and appeal to them. Ideas may impress people; sentiments help to stimulate them.

A list of specific sentiments to which you might appeal would, of course, be endless. The following list is given only to serve as a starting place for a list of your own:

1. Acquisition, thrift, and saving.
2. Adventure and romance.
3. Altruism.
4. Companionship.
5. Competition, opposition, and fighting.
6. Conformity and imitation.
7. Cooperation.
8. Creativity.
9. Giving.
10. Independence, self-reliance, individualism.
11. Loyalty.
12. Power.
13. Prejudice.
14. Reverence, respect, worship.
15. Sacrifice.
16. Security.

Emotions. Sentiments are composite mental attitudes which, once formed, are relatively permanent and consistent in an individual; emotions, on the other hand, are more transitory and vary greatly from time to time in the individual. You may tend to be "conservative" or "liberal" in your general attitude, but you will feel happy at one time, and angry at still another time. Emotions are feelings, impulses, passions, states of mind, and they come and go.

Although it is true that our emotions are variable, they are not unimportant. Our passions color our judgment and affect our decisions; what we believe and what we do are in large measure determined by what we feel. Human beings are not disembodied brains or objective computers; we care, we feel, we respond. And often, on the depth of these responses, depends the depth of our commitments.

Inspiring, then, depends not only on appealing to established sentiments, but on arousing strong emotional responses. You must, to put the matter in current jargon, get your audience "involved." Without drippy sentimentality, without "corniness," and without blatant excesses, you must make your hearers care about your subject.

But how can you elicit the feelings you want? There are no simple magical answers, but there are two important suggestions: (1) decide what specific response you want at given points in the speech, and (2) choose carefully the wording or the device that will be most likely to produce the desired result. Any list of emotions to which you might appeal would be incomplete, but the following list ought to help you to begin the compilation of a list of your own:

1. Affection.	17. Fear.
2. Anger.	18. Grief or sorrow.
3. Anxiety.	19. Hate.
4. Ardor.	20. Hope.
5. Attraction and allurement.	21. Impatience.
6. Concern.	22. Irritation.
7. Contempt.	23. Joy.
8. Courage.	24. Love.
9. Curiosity.	25. Pity.
10. Desire.	26. Pleasure, satisfaction, gratification, enjoyment, thrill.
11. Devotion.	27. Pride.
12. Discomfort.	28. Resentment.
13. Disgust.	29. Revulsion.
14. Dislike.	30. Sympathy.
15. Enthusiasm.	31. Zeal.
16. Excitement.	

These are the materials of which the rally speech is constructed, sentiments and emotions which set the fundamental drives in motion. And the sources of these materials are in the audience. Your task as speaker is to analyze the audience and select the appropriate appeals.

Organization. Like any address, the rally speech has an introduction that gains the attention, interest, sympathy, and respect of the audience, a body that develops the central theme fully and effectively, and a conclusion that brings the development to a climax.

The introduction should relate the theme to the audience and occasion. You may want to begin with a striking statement of your theme or some reference to establish a common ground with the audience. You may begin with a relevant illustration or quotation. In any case, your introduction should be arresting and appropriate.

In the body of the speech you will develop your central theme, which will ordinarily be some variation on the formulas: "_____ should be supported (or approved, respected, revered, praised)" or "_____ deserves our wholehearted, steadfast devotion (or loyalty, support, commitment.)" Keep the central idea clearly in mind in planning the divisions of the body, and include no portion unless it is directly related to supporting the principal theme. Avoid tangents and digressions. Concentrate on amplifying and augmenting your one point. You could organize the divisions around the reasons for support or devotion, around the results of loyalty that will accrue, or around means of expressing commitment and putting it into action. You might also, in a brief rally speech, develop your theme through a series of illustrations, descriptions, or analogies that vividly portray for your audience the need for active participation and support.

The speaker at a rally should leave his listeners with a strong "punch"; the speech should build to a climax. Your purpose is to intensify attitudes and feelings, to move the audience. The conclusion must not be a let-down but a stirring appeal. Whether you use a direct appeal, a vivid illustration, or an apt, moving quotation, you should select your conclusion carefully and prepare it thoroughly. Your closing statements should be the high point of audience attention, interest, and enthusiasm.

Adaptation, style, and other distinctives

A basic principle of effective speaking is that the speaker's language must be adjusted to the purpose, audience, and occasion. Such adaptation is essential to the success of the rally speech. You cannot intensify feelings with drab wording; you cannot move men to active participation and vigorous support with vague generalities and hazy abstractions; you cannot stir hearts with words that are unfamiliar, impersonal, or offensive. Your words must be direct, clear, vivid, and in good taste.

At the rally, you are face-to-face with your audience. Talk to them; talk with them! In writing, you cannot speak directly to your readers, and you are likely to use the impersonal "one does this" and "one says that." But in speaking, the impersonal pronoun seems distant and cold. Use the personal pronouns **we, I,** and **you.** Far better to say "you and I know" than "one knows"!

Audiences will not respond (at least as you want them to do) to words that they do not understand. Your words must be clear. Use the short word in preference to the long one; use the familiar word in preference to the esoteric one; use the simple word in place of the difficult one. It is better to say "words of many syllables" than "polysyllabic words." Use words that are concrete and specific rather than those that are general and abstract. Use concrete nouns and active verbs. Say "General Westmoreland" instead of saying "a certain American general," and instead of saying "it has been disclosed in discourse by the President," say "the President said."

You should use language that is vivid and colorful. Your words should produce images in the minds of your listeners. Through your choice of language, you should make your problem, your cause, or your need so real, so firsthand to your audience that it thinks it can see it, hear it, taste it, smell it, or touch it. Why tell an audience "there are multitudes of people on welfare in New York City" when you can tell it "welfare recipients in New York City outnumber the inhabitants of the city of Louisville" or "if you put all the welfare recipients of New York City together you would have to build a city larger than Louisville to house them"? Why tell hearers "the slums are unfit for human beings" when you can tell them that "all one little girl wants this Christmas is to get rid of the large, vicious rats in her apartment"? If you want to arouse disgust and revulsion, why say "the buildings are dirty" when you can describe halls that "reek of urine and vomit and unemptied garbage"? It would be more effective to describe the screams and moans of an injured young Negro whom a physician on duty in the emergency room looked at, listened to, and refused to help, than to say "I know a typical doctor who was unfaithful to his oath."

Your language should reflect your good taste. Use slang only when it is necessary to contribute to your purpose; avoid profanity; and abstain from the very appearance of obscenity. Harry Truman, you may remember, used a mild curse in one of his rally speeches in Texas during the 1960 presidential campaign and was severely criticized for it. Do not get carried away. Keep your words well within the bounds of good taste.

Your phrases should be striking and fresh, and your sentences should be rather short. Martin Luther King's stirring speech at the March on Washington is best remembered for the memorable phrase he repeated several times: "I have a dream!" A brief, catchy slogan may be used to advantage in a rally speech. You should remember that (1) a new, fresh slogan or a new twist on a familiar slogan is more effective than the repetition of a cliché, and (2) slogans, when overdone or overused, can work against your purpose.

Use illustrations. Clothe your ideas in human details and in appropriate, moving stories. Illustrations bring concepts down to the level of our common experience; they bring truths home to us. They are an important and useful device in inspiring audiences.

These, then, are the attributes of good oral style adapted for the rally speech: words that are direct, clear, vivid, and tasteful; phrases that strike the listener as fresh and memorable; and illustrations that are appropriate and moving.

Presentation

Your delivery of an address at a rally should leave two major impressions: conviction and control. Through your manner of speaking, you should convey that you yourself care about the topic. Your voice, your stance, your movement, your facial expressions should all transmit your deep concern and your own commitment. Be dynamic; be vigorous; be enthusiastic. But be controlled. Excesses in delivery detract from your effectiveness. You can be dynamic without constant movement; you can be vigorous without shouting; you can be enthusiastic without losing your composure. Keep your own emotions and the display of your feelings within reasonable limits. Undisciplined emotionalism is related to restrained feeling as a flood is to irrigation:

too much of a good thing produces more damage than benefit! Use your heart, but don't lose your head!

Specimen speech

On August 28, 1963, before a multitude of more than 200,000 black and white advocates of civil rights assembled from all over the nation at the Lincoln Memorial in Washington, D. C., Dr. Martin Luther King delivered his now famous "I Have a Dream Speech." One of a number of speakers, Dr. King was the one who captured the mood of the throng and spoke most effectively to their hearts.

The "Dream Speech" offers an excellent example of the use of emotional appeals in a rally speech. What the address lacks in structure, it makes up in style and pathos.

The **N.Y. Amsterdam News** of September 17, 1966, reprinted the speech and included these comments on it:

> Dr. King had a prepared text, just as did the numerous other nationally known persons who stepped to the rostrum. But soon after he began to speak it became clear to all that he was emotionally moved, and those who knew him well had the feeling that he would not long stick to his prepared text.
>
> He didn't.
>
> He had only been speaking a short time when he put aside his prepared text and started to speak from his heart as a Baptist minister and a Negro looking to the dream of America.
>
> When he finished, the huge throng of 200,000, which had been called the most orderly multitude in history, burst into a crescendo of applause that reverberated from the Lincoln Memorial to the Nation's Capitol. It was a historic moment.

The text of Dr. King's speech, which follows, is taken from the recording, "The March on Washington," released by the Council for United Civil Rights Leadership. The speech is reprinted here with Dr. King's permission and with the permission of Joan Daves. (Copyright © 1963 by Martin Luther King, Jr.)

> I am happy to join with you today in what will go down in history as the greatest demonstration for freedom in the history of our nation. Five score years ago, a great American in whose symbolic shadow we stand today, signed the Emancipation Proclamation. This momentous decree came as a

great beacon light of hope to millions of Negro slaves who had been seared in the flames of withering injustice; it came as a joyous daybreak to end the long night of their captivity.

But one hundred years later the Negro still is not free. One hundred years later, the life of the Negro is still sadly crippled by the manacles of segregation and the chains of discrimination. One hundred years later, the Negro lives on a lonely island of poverty in the midst of a vast ocean of material prosperity. One hundred years later, the Negro is still languished in the corners of American society and finds himself an exile in his own land.

And so we have come here today to dramatize a shameful condition. In a sense we have come to our nation's capital to cash a check. When the architects of our republic wrote the magnificent words of the Constitution and the Declaration of Independence, they were signing a promissory note to which every American was to fall heir. This note was a promise that all men—black men as well as white men—would be guaranteed the inalienable rights of life, liberty, and the pursuit of happiness. It is obvious today that America has defaulted on this promissory note insofar as her citizens of color are concerned. Instead of honoring this sacred obligation, America has given the Negro a bad check—a check which has come back marked "insufficient funds." But we refuse to believe that the bank of justice is bankrupt! We refuse to believe that there are insufficient funds in the great vaults of opportunity of this nation! And so we have come to cash this check. A check that will give us upon demand the riches of freedom and the security of justice.

We have also come to this hallowed spot to remind America of the fierce urgency of **now**. This is no time to engage in the luxury of cooling off or to take the tranquilizing drug of gradualism. Now is the time to make real the promises of democracy; now is the time to rise from the dark and desolate valley of segregation to the sunlit path of racial justice; now is the time to rise from the quicksands of racial injustice to the solid rock of brotherhood; now is the time to make justice a reality for all of God's children.

It would be fatal for the nation to overlook the urgency of the moment. This sweltering summer of the Negro's legitimate discontent will not pass until there is an invigorating autumn of freedom and equality. 1963 is not an end, but a beginning. Those who hope that the Negro needed to blow off steam and will now be content will have a rude awakening if the nation returns to business as usual. There will be neither rest nor tranquility in America until the Negro is granted his citizenship rights. The whirlwinds of revolt will continue to shake the foundations of our nation until the bright day of justice emerges.

But there is something that I must say to my people who stand on the warm threshold which leads into the palace of justice. In the process of gaining our rightful place, we must not be guilty of wrongful deeds. Let us not seek to satisfy our thirst for freedom by drinking from the cup of bitterness and hatred. We must forever conduct our struggle on the high plane of dignity and discipline. We must not allow our creative protest to degenerate into physical violence. Again and again, we must rise to the majestic heights of meeting physical force with soul force. The marvelous new militancy which has engulfed the Negro community must not lead us to a distrust of all white people, for many of our white brothers, as evidenced by their presence here today, have come to realize that their destiny is part of the marchers'. They have come to realize that their freedom is inextricably bound to our freedom; we cannot walk alone.

And as we walk, we must make the pledge that we shall always march ahead. We cannot turn back. There are those who are asking the devotées of civil rights, "When will you be satisfied?" We can never be satisfied as long as the Negro is the victim of the unspeakable horrors of police brutality. We can never be satisfied as long as our bodies, heavy with the fatigue of travel, cannot gain lodging in the motels of the highways and the hotels of the cities. We cannot be satisfied as long as the Negro's basic mobility is from a smaller ghetto to a larger one. We can never be satisfied as long as our children are stripped of their selfhood and robbed of their dignity by signs stating FOR WHITES ONLY. We cannot be satisfied as long as the Negro in Mississippi cannot vote and the Negro in New York believes he has nothing for which to vote. No—no, we are not satisfied, and **we will not** be satisfied until "justice rolls down like waters and righteousness like a mighty stream."

I am not unmindful that some of you have come here out of great trials and tribulations. Some of you have come fresh from narrow jail cells. Some of you have come from areas where your quest for freedom left you battered by the storms of persecution and staggered by the winds of police brutality. You have been the veterans of creative suffering. Continue to work with the faith that honor in suffering is redemptive. Go back to Mississippi; go back to Alabama; go back to South Carolina; go back to Georgia; go back to Louisiana; go back to the slums and ghettos of our northern cities, knowing that somehow this situation can and will be changed. Let us not wallow in the valley of despair.

I say to you today, my friends, so even though we face the difficulties of today and tomorrow, I still have a dream. It is a dream deeply rooted in the American dream. I have a dream that one day this nation will rise up and live out the true meaning of its creed: "We hold these truths to be self-evident—that all men are created equal." I have a dream that one day on the red hills of Georgia the sons of former slaves and the sons of former slaveowners will there be able to sit down together at the table of brotherhood. I have a dream that one day even the state of Mississippi, a state sweltering with the heat of injustice, sweltering with the heat of oppression, will be transformed into an oasis of freedom and justice. I have a dream that my four little children will one day live in a nation where they will not be judged by the color of their skin but by the content of their character. I have a dream today. I have a dream that one day down in Alabama, with its vicious racists, with its governor having his lips dripping with the words of interposition and nullification—one day right there in Alabama—little black boys and black girls will be able to join hands with little white boys and white girls as sisters and brothers. I have a dream today. I have a dream that one day "every valley shall be exalted; every hill and mountain shall be made low; the rough places will be made plain and the crooked places will be made straight and the glory of The Lord shall be revealed and all flesh shall see it together."

This is our hope; this is the faith that I go back to the South with. With this faith, we will be able to hew out of the mountain of despair a stone of hope. With this faith, we will be able to transform the jangling discords of our nation into a beautiful symphony of brotherhood. With this faith, we will be able to work together, to pray together, to struggle together, to go to jail together, to stand up for freedom together—knowing that we **will** be free one day. This will be the day when all of God's children will be able to sing with new meaning:

> My country 'tis of thee,
> Sweet land of liberty,
> Of thee I sing,
> Land where my Fathers died,
> Land of the Pilgrim's pride,
> From every mountainside
> Let freedom ring.

And if America is to be a great nation, this must become true.

And so, **let freedom ring** from the prodigious hilltops of New Hampshire; let freedom ring from the mighty mountains of New York; let freedom ring from the heightening Alleghenies of Pennsylvania; let freedom ring from the snow-capped Rockies of Colorado; let freedom ring from the curvaceous slopes of California. But not only that! Let freedom ring from Stone Mountain of Georgia; let freedom ring from Lookout Mountain of Tennessee; let freedom ring from every hill and molehill of Mississippi! From **every** mountainside, let freedom ring! And when it happens, when we allow freedom's ring; when we let it ring from every village and every hamlet, from every state and every city, we will be able to speed up that day when all of God's children, black men and white men, Jews and Gentiles, Protestants and Catholics, will be able to join hands and sing in the words of the old Negro spiritual:

> Free at last,
> Free at last,
> Thank God Almighty
> We're free at last!

Questions for specimen speech analysis

1. Remembering the limited objectives of a rally speech, would you expect Dr. King to present new or unusual ideas in his address? In your judgment, was the topic appropriate for the audience and occasion?

2. Was there a single, unifying theme to Dr. King's message? Can his address be summarized in one sentence? If so, what is that central idea?

3. Were there digressions and tangents from the central theme? If so, were they distracting? Did they hamper the effectiveness of the speech?

4. Were the supporting materials chosen with the purpose of stimulation in mind?

5. Did the speaker seek to utilize the basic drives of his audience? On what basis did you reach your conclusion?

6. To what sentiments did Dr. King appeal? How direct were those appeals? How effective?

7. To what emotions did Dr. King appeal? Were the emotional appeals tastefully and tactfully handled? If you had been present, would they have moved you? Did Dr. King ever lapse into sentimentality or overuse of emotion?

8. Did Dr. King use logic or evidence for supporting materials? What kinds of reasoning did he employ? How strong were the figurative analogies?

9. Was the introduction fitting? Did it make the theme sufficiently clear? Was the conclusion appropriate? Was it a moving climax or a disappointing anticlimax? Did the conclusion restate the theme in a fresh and memorable way?

10. Was the body of the speech divided into balanced parts? Were there smooth transitions? Was the progression of thought logical and easy to follow? Was there any consistent pattern to the body? If so, what was it?

11. Was the language of the speech suited to the purpose, audience, and occasion? Was Dr. King's language clear, direct, and vivid?

12. Was the wording in good taste? Did Dr. King manage to avoid clichés? Did some of the language reflect stereotyped thinking?

13. Did Dr. King clothe his ideas in human details? Did his words "bring truths home"?

14. Were there striking phrases? Did the use of parallelism, repetition, and refrain enhance the style?

15. Were the allusions and quotations effectively managed? Did they contribute to the purpose of inspiration? Were they always clearly relevant logically?

16. Remembering that the goal of a rally speech is limited to inspiring the faithful, how would you evaluate Dr. King's address?

FOUR

Social occasions: entertaining

The after-dinner speech

Purpose

From time to time, men gather for fun and fellowship, and speakers are expected to contribute to the atmosphere with speeches to entertain. Although your speech may convey information, transmit judgments, and touch the emotions, your principal purpose in the entertaining speech is to interest, please, and amuse your listeners. The response you want from your audience is enjoyment. You should remember, however, that your speech may be enjoyable—and therefore entertaining—without producing convulsive laughter. The speaker, even in the speech to entertain, is still a speaker and not a comic.

Occasion

Speeches to entertain are most often given on social occasions, times of conviviality and comradeship. Even the most conservative approve of socializing, when "socializing" connotes friendliness, hospitality, welcome, and enjoyment. The social situations where speechmaking is done are usually either parties or meals. The parties may vary from informal get-togethers and smokers to formal receptions, and "after-dinner speaking" may be in order after any meal—whether a wedding breakfast, a club luncheon, a church supper, or a banquet.

You should remember, if you are to speak at a social occasion, that pleasure in human companionship has drawn your listeners together and that your task is to contribute to the climate of good-fellowship. Be brief. Especially after your audience has consumed a meal, be brief. Your drowsy, dyspeptic hearers are sure to believe that brevity is the soul of wit.

Preparation

Like marriage, the speech to entertain should not be entered into lightly. Entertaining is serious business; it should be approached as any other form of public address, with careful planning and thorough preparation. In fact, speeches to entertain are most difficult to prepare and present, and you should not be misled into thinking their development easy simply because successful speakers appear at ease while giving them.

The speech to entertain, like any speech, must have a central theme. After analyzing the prospective audience and the occasion, you must decide on a single, unified idea for your speech. You must ask yourself, "What is the ONE POINT I wish to make?" Phrase that theme in one complete, declarative, affirmative, appropriate sentence.

Until the statement of your central theme is formulated, you cannot efficiently, systematically, and logically gather materials or organize them. The central theme is the test of inclusion or exclusion of materials; you must include everything necessary to expound the idea fully, and you must exclude everything (no matter how funny or appealing to you) that is not an integral part of that theme. Likewise, the central theme dictates the organization of your materials; your structure is found by dividing the idea into parallel, coordinate, equal, logical parts, and each division must be clearly related to the central theme of the speech.

There are two steps in formulating the summary statement for your speech: (1) selecting the subject, the topic of your speech and (2) selecting the predicate, the focus of your speech. The subject, of course, is what you are going to talk about, and the predicate is what you are going to say about that subject. Phrasing a summary statement is necessary for the preparation of **any** speech, but inexperienced speakers are most likely to omit this element in devising speeches to entertain.

Topics. Almost any topic can be handled with good humor and in good taste. But the subject should be carefully chosen. It should be appropriate for the speaker, for the audience, and for the occasion.

A topic could be appropriate for the speaker either because it is already associated in the minds of the audience with the speaker or because it is out of keeping with the speaker's known interests, capabilities, or character. A topic, then, could be fitting for the speaker if it is related to or incongruous with the speaker's reputation.

A subject would be especially appropriate for the audience if it contained two basic elements: (1) something familiar and (2) a surprise. Audiences will be amused only by what they understand, and they will understand only what they find familiar. References to people, events, and situations about which the audience knows nothing, no matter how clever, will not entertain an audience. Your hearers will appreciate what they know and recognize as funny. To suit your listeners, not only must your topic be a subject about which they already have information, it must take them somewhat by surprise. The unexpected twist is a necessary ingredient for concocting a topic to the taste of your audience.

Keep the occasion in mind when selecting your topic. The nature of the occasion, the place of the meeting, or the time or circumstances of the gathering may suggest a particular kind of topic. Barry Goldwater, for example, gave a delightful imitation of the typical convention speech at a mock political convention. Of course, the topic was appropriate for him and for his audience of young people interested in politics, but the occasion dictated the kind of approach he took in his hilarious satire.

The key word in choosing a subject for a speech to entertain is **propriety.** Just ask yourself, **"Is it appropriate**—for me, for my listeners, for that time and place?"

Materials. The phrase "a sense of humor" is used generally by the public to denote the ability to perceive or appreciate the comic, the ability to see something funny. Critics, however, have tended to distinguish between the two basic materials of speeches to entertain— humor and wit.

Although both humor and wit produce amusement through use of incongruity and surprise, there are subtle differences between them. Humor **describes** the subject and **delights** the audience; wit **exposes** the subject and **diverts** the audience. Humor is sustained, deep, natural, and usually kindly; wit is brief, sudden, sharp, artful, and sometimes severe. Humor arises from accident; wit arises from the speaker's quick perception and ingenuity. And there is a difference in the nature of the comment as well: humor is the more emotional of the two and wit the more intellectual.

If one accepts this distinction between humor and wit, he will probably agree with the generalization of Arthur M. Schlesinger, Jr. that "Roosevelt was a man of humor, Kennedy a man of wit." He might also agree that Adlai Stevenson was that rare speaker who utilized humor and wit with equal effectiveness.

Humor. The first of the two basic materials you can use for the speech to entertain is humor, which usually relies on one of three devices: jokes, anecdotes, or "punch lines". Jokes are funny, apocryphal stories; anecdotes are brief, amusing historical or biographical accounts, usually personal in nature; "punch lines" are ludicrous remarks that come as a jolting contrast to the preceding buildup.

Beware of "canned" humor; ready-made jokes usually fall flat. Most of us groan, at least inwardly, when a speaker begins, "That reminds me of a story . . ." and feel like walking out if the speaker rattles off jests he heard, as we also heard, on a recent TV variety show. The temptation to rely on tired jokes borrowed from comedians—both amateur and professional—is not new. Cicero warned that jests which do not arise from the situation naturally are awkward and frigid. If you do use a joke, be certain that it is tailored for the particular audience and occasion and that it is fresh.

President Kennedy rarely told jokes, but before a friendly audience at the AFL-CIO Convention in December 1961, he applied a joke to Secretary of Labor Goldberg, who was present at the meeting with him.

> I am delighted to be here with you and with the Secretary of Labor, Arthur Goldberg. I was up in New York, stressing physical fitness, and in line with that, Arthur went over with a group to Switzerland to climb some of the mountains there. They got up about five and he was in bed. He got up to join them later and when they all came back at four o'clock in the afternoon he didn't come back with them.

> So they sent out search parties and there was not a sign that afternoon and night. The next day, the Red Cross went out and around, calling: "Goldberg, Goldberg, it's the Red Cross!" Then this voice came down from the mountain, "I gave at the office!"

President Kennedy adapted the story to the situation, to himself, and to his friend on the platform. The joke was appropriate and well-received.

Anecdotes, introduced to illustrate a point, can be used quite successfully to express an idea in human terms. Many listeners seem to understand and appreciate generalizations best when they come in the form of stories about particular people in specific situations. Alben Barkley, Adlai Stevenson, and Brooks Hays utilized such stories with great effectiveness. The following anecdote is typical of the distinctive, folksy humor of Mr. Hays:

> I'm not afraid of experts. I was sitting by a couple in Washington at a dinner party one night when the man who had just met the lady said to her, "And you're Mrs. Post?" And she said yes. "Mrs. Emily Post?" And she said yes. "Well, Mrs. Post, you're eating my salad!"

Much of the humor of both jokes and anecdotes may be found in the climactic final statement—the "punch line". But the "punch line", the unexpected twist that jars the listeners' expectations and jolts them into amusement, may come after some other form of build-up rather than a joke or anecdote. You may, with a series of statements, lead your audience to think you are going to say one thing and instead say something entirely different. If the expectations are high enough, if the surprise is great enough, and if the punch is timed well enough, you should provoke your listeners into mirth.

Wit. The second of the two basic materials of entertaining speeches is wit, which is the product of the speaker's or writer's imagination and cleverness. Wit may take the form of puns, double-entendres, malapropisms, quips, banter, satire, parody, raillery, understatement, overstatement, and irony.

The word **pun** comes from an Italian word meaning "fine point" and denotes word-play arising from homonyms, words which sound alike but differ in meaning. We have all heard the wornout deprecation that "puns are the lowest form of humor", but we have also observed that some of the greatest speakers have used them effectively. If the word-play is clever and the two meanings are readily clear to the audience, you might include the pun in your speech. If you are in doubt about using any particular pun, omit it; many audiences react with loud groans to poor puns they think "corny".

Adlai Stevenson used puns successfully in a campaign speech in Brooklyn in 1952:

> Now, as usual, my friends, the pre-election thunder comes from the Republicans. They control most of the nation's newspapers and magazines. They have the slickest slogans and the shiniest posters. They win most of the pre-election polls, and sometimes they win them in a Gallup. It's not a very good pun, but it's the best I could do.
>
> Then, the people will vote on Tuesday. I understand that on Monday the newspapers plan to publish a "five-star final."[1]

A double entendre is a particular kind of pun; it relies, like any other pun, on ambiguity for its humor, but one of the possible meanings is risqué. I do not recommend the use of double entendres in a speech. Good humor should be in good taste. The speaker who warned girls not to return from a sit-in as a virgin made may have been funny, but he was also gauche (or as many collegians would have it, "gross").

A malapropism is a ridiculous misuse of a word; usually it involves the substitution of an incorrect word for another word which it resembles in sound. If the unexpected (incorrect) word is carefully chosen, adequately stressed, and genuinely funny, this device might be successful. You may decide for yourself about the success of the effort of the speaker who asserted that "the Republican Party produced a great **defect** on the United States".

Quips are short, sharp sallies and can be delightful witticisms. John Kennedy was a master of this form of wit. To students working temporarily in Washington he commented: "Sometimes I wish I had a summer job here." When he pushed the switch to activate the Green River generators he said, "I never know when I press these whether I am going to blow up Massachusetts or start the project." The new plant was one hundred fifty miles from the button-pushing ceremony, and confirmation that the generators had been successfully started was to come over the loudspeaker. While waiting for the announcement, Kennedy quipped: "If we don't hear from him, it's back to the drawing boards!"

Probably the most famous of Kennedy's quips is his introduction of himself as the man who accompanied Jacqueline Kennedy to Paris. My favorite Kennedy quip, however, did not occur in a public speech, but was reported by some of his associates. After the disastrous invasion of the Bay of Pigs, the President was informed that the Gallup Poll showed his popularity had reached an all-time high. He exclaimed, ". . . it's as bad as Eisenhower! The worse I do the more popular I get!"

[1] Bill Adler, ed. **The Stevenson Wit** (New York: Doubleday, 1965).

Quips are brief, snappy jests or jibes; to be successful they must arise naturally from the speaker's personality and imagination. Sharp remarks are, necessarily, dependent for their production on sharp thinking; it takes a bright mind to produce bright retorts. But you must take care to deliver the sallies with good humor, good taste, and goodwill; you do not want to be thought a smart aleck.

Ridicule, which can be an effectively devastating kind of wit, may take three forms. The three vary in degree of severity and in purpose. Banter is mild ridicule; it playfully teases its object. Satire is carica-ture; it exaggerates the distinctive features of its object. Raillery is scornful ridicule; it subjects its object to sarcasm or contempt.

Banter is mild, playful teasing. Many successful after-dinner speakers begin with some jests for fun, adapted to the audience and occasion, which are used to disarm and warm the listeners. Banter is always friendly, never malicious. Your banter should combine clever-ness, propriety, and lightness.

President John Kennedy was a master of banter. Speaking before the Newspaper Publishers Association, he teased about their failure to support him in his campaign for the Presidency:

> I have selected as the title of my remarks tonight "The President and the Press." Some may suggest that this would be more naturally worded "The President Versus the Press" but those are not my sentiments to-night. It is true, however, that when a well-known diplomat from another country demanded recently that our State Department repudiate certain newspaper attacks on his colleagues, it was unnecessary for us to reply that this Administration was not responsible for the press, for the press had already made it clear that it was not responsible for this Administration.

In his commencement address before the cadets at West Point, Kennedy bantered:

> I want to say that I wish all of you the greatest success. While I say that, I am not unmindful of the fact that two graduates of this Academy have reached the White House and neither was a member of my party. Until I'm more certain that this trend will be broken, I wish that all of you may be generals and not Commander-in-Chief.

Ridicule, of course, is a two-sided sword; it can cut both ways. The speaker can turn it on himself. In fact, some of the best banter is pro-duced by those who do not take themselves too seriously, are able to laugh at themselves, and are willing to have an audience join in the fun. Kennedy greeted the convention of the AFL-CIO with these words of appreciation: "I want to express my pleasure at this invitation as one whose work and continuity of employment has depended in part upon the union movement." The following example of self-ridiculing banter is from President Kennedy's speech before the Newspaper Publishers Association:

> On the other hand, I realize that your staff and wire service photographers may be complaining that they do not enjoy the same green privileges at the local golf courses which they once did. It is true that my predecessor did not object as I do to pictures of one's golfing skill in action. But neither, on the other hand, did he ever bean a Secret Service man!

Through exaggeration of details, satire holds up to ridicule vices, follies, stupidities, abuses, absurdities, and idiosyncracies. Satire depends upon distortion; certain elements or aspects are played up to heighten the effect. Like a cartoonist who draws features out of proportion to emphasize them, the satirist achieves his derisive purpose by selecting distinctive details and mockingly overstating them. To be successful, the imitation in the burlesque must be faithful enough to the original to be recognizable, but the absurdities in the travesty must be exaggerated enough to be ludicrous.

One technique you may find useful is to treat serious things as comic and comic things as serious, important things as trivial and trivial things as profound. Mock dignity and gravity, when applied to trifles, and slighting unconcern or irreverence, when applied to the respected and hallowed, amuses audiences through shocking incongruity. One student convulsed his audience by giving a solemn eulogy to a dead fly, and Tom Lehrer's impertinence delighted his listeners when he observed that it would take "twenty billion dollars of your money to put some clown on the moon."

Satire can be an effective weapon. You may use it not only to point out errors and shortcomings; you may use it to gain support for change and reform. Remember, then, that the spirit of your burlesque should be that of taunting and twitting, not degrading and damning.

Raillery is pointed ridicule; it usually contains an element of sarcasm and scorn. Through raillery, a more direct attack than either banter or satire, you may employ your wit to fashion barbs with which to needle opponents or puncture opposing views. If you do use this form of ridicule, be careful to apply the cutting edge of your words deftly. It is better to needle than to knife; your aim is to prod your hearers into amusement and contempt, not to provoke them into sympathy for whatever you intend to ridicule.

In his keynote address at the Democratic National Convention in 1956, Governor Frank Clement ridiculed the administration of President Dwight D. Eisenhower. He projected the impending exodus, after the certain Republican defeat, as follows:

> Yes, we are met here tonight to plan for the happy hour when representatives of the party of the people shall be restored to direction of the National Government—and when the opposition party of privilege and pillage passes over the Potomac in the greatest water-crossing since the children of Israel crossed the Red Sea.
>
> How different, however, will be the fate of the parties to this mass exodus.
>
> Where the children of Israel had only Moses to lead them on, the evacuation of January, 1957, will be an astronomer's dream of shooting stars, for this trek will have generals to the left of 'em, generals to the right of 'em, generals in front of them as these old soldiers fold their political tents and just fade away.[2]

A parody is a speech written in the characteristic style of some other speech or speaker. Parody offers some excellent opportunities for clever development of a theme. The humor lies in the audience's recognition of the original being imitated and in its appreciation of the devices used in the imitation. One of my students presented an uproarious parody of Marc Antony's oration at the dinner which closed the class in public speaking; the course was substituted for the corpse, and I was substituted for Brutus. ("The noble King hath told you that the course was beneficial, and King is an honorable man!")

The funniest, and most vicious, parody I know is Oliver Jensen's "Gettysburg Address in Eisenhowerese." Anyone who is familiar both with the noble language of Lincoln's original and with Eisenhower's foggy prose style will find this merciless imitation exceedingly accurate—and hilarious.

> I haven't checked these figures but 87 years ago, I think it was, a number of individuals organized a governmental set-up here in this country, I believe it covered certain Eastern areas, with this idea they were following up based on a sort of national independence arrangement and the program that every individual is just as good as every other individual. Well, now, of course, we are dealing with this big difference of opinion,

[2] Frank G. Clement, "Keynote Address," **Vital Speeches of the Day,** XXII (September 1, 1956), 674.

civil disturbance you might say, although I don't like to appear to take sides or name any individuals, and the point is naturally to check up, by actual experience in the field, to see whether any governmental set-up with a basis like the one I was mentioning has any validity and find out whether that dedication by those early individuals will pay off in lasting values and things of that kind.

Well, here we are, at the scene where one of these disturbances between different sides got going. We want to pay our tribute to those loved ones, those departed individuals who made the supreme sacrifice here on the basis of their opinions about how this thing ought to be handled. And I would say this. It is absolutely in order to do this.

But if you look at the over-all picture of this, we can't pay any tribute— we can't sanctify this area, you might say—we can't hallow according to whatever individual creeds or faiths or sort of religious outlooks are involved like I said about this particular area. It was those individuals themselves, including the enlisted men, very brave individuals, who have given this religious character to the area. The way I see it, the rest of the world will not remember any statements issued here but it will never forget how these men put their shoulders to the wheel and carried this idea down the fairway.

Now frankly, our job, the living individuals' job here, is to pick up the burden and sink the putt they made these big efforts here for. It is our job to get on with the assignment—and from these deceased fine individuals to take extra inspiration, you could call it, for the same theories about the set-up for which they made such a big contribution. We have to make up our minds right here and now, as I see it, that they didn't put out all that blood, perspiration and—well—that they didn't just make a dry run here, and that all of us here, under God, that is, the God of our choice, shall beef up this idea about freedom and liberty and those kind of arrangements, and that government of all individuals, by all individuals and for the individuals, shall not pass out of the world-picture.[3]

Exaggeration for the sake of effect is a common occurrence in everyday conversation; hyperbole simply underscores the point to be made. For example, the student who commented that the professor was older than Methuselah did not expect to be taken literally. Exaggeration, or overstatement, is also a common form of witticism. You may magnify reality, stretch the truth, and heighten the details; the overdrawn picture can entertain your listeners. President Kennedy somewhat over-

[3] Dwight MacDonald, ed. **Parodies** (New York: Random House, 1960), 447–448. Copyrighted by Oliver Jensen. Reprinted with the permission of the author.

stated the narrow margin by which he was elected: "Three years ago and one week, by a landslide, the people of the United States elected me to the Presidency of this country."

Listeners are often surprised into mirth by a statement or word that is weaker than they expected. Moderation may be not only a virtue, it may be a delight if properly handled. Build your hearers' expectations up, lead them to think only a strong word or statement is appropriate, and then give the mild anticlimax. Use a tame word when truth dictates a vigorous one and a bland phrase when accuracy demands a powerful one.

The explorer was employing understatement when he said, "I take great pride in my sense of direction. One of the most important attributes of a successful explorer is that he can always find his way. I myself have never been lost; in twenty years of expeditions I have never been lost. Of course, I have been bewildered for a month or two!"

One of Kennedy's best-known understatements is his answer to the question of how he became a war hero. He said, "It was absolutely involuntary. They sank my boat." To the publishers, Mr. Kennedy commented, "If in the last few months, your White House reporters and photographers have been attending church services with regularity, that has surely done them no harm!"

Saying one thing and meaning the opposite is called irony. The humor lies in the contrast between what is said (the literal words) and what is really thought (the implied meaning). To be successful, the speaker's actual intention must be clear to the audience, the situations, things, or people about whom he speaks must be familiar to the audience, and the points made must in themselves be funny.

To convey the ironic meaning you must carefully select the phrasing of your ideas and you must select the appropriate intonation pattern. Generally, you will use more circumflex inflections than usual to carry the implied meanings. You ordinarily will not deliver irony in a matter-of-fact voice.

Schlesinger says of President Kennedy that "irony was his most distinctive mode of wit." Typical of Kennedy's irony is the following excerpt from a speech at the University of California at Berkeley on March 1, 1962:

> The last time that I came to this stadium was twenty-two years ago, when I visited it in November of 1940 as a student at a nearby small school for the game with Stanford. I must say I had a much warmer

reception today than I did on that occasion. In those days, we used to fill these universities for football, and now we do it for academic events, and I'm not sure that this doesn't represent a rather dangerous trend for the future of our country.

These, then, are the basic materials of entertaining—humor and wit. Sources of humor you will find in the world around you—in your experiences, in the experiences of your acquaintances, and in your observations. The source of wit is your ingenuity; you create witty remarks from your perception of the incongruous and the unlikely.

Do not rely for the materials of your speeches on joke books or books for toastmasters. Simply look in you and around you; there is plenty of material for many speeches to entertain.

Organization. A speech to entertain is a speech. The sentence may seem repetitious and simple, but the concept is an important one. An entertaining speech, like any other speech, is carefully prepared; an entertaining speech, like any other speech, has a central idea; an entertaining speech, like any other speech, is partitioned into divisions; an entertaining speech, like any other speech, has an introduction, a body, and a conclusion. In brief, an entertaining speech, like any other speech, is organized, and its development can easily be followed by the audience.

Too many inexperienced speakers think that the speech to entertain is just a comic routine, and that the entertaining speaker need only imitate stand-up comedians who are successful in night clubs or on television. Nothing could be further from the truth! A succession of jokes strung together loosely or a barrage of unrelated, though funny, Bob Hope quips is not a speech. What is appropriate for a night club or for television is not appropriate for the banquet hall or the luncheon table. When a speech is expected, give a speech—not a routine!

The other most common misunderstanding of the inexperienced speaker is the mistaken belief that one anecdote doth a speech make. An anecdote is an illustration, but it is not a speech. One long "shaggy dog story" about "the funniest thing that ever happened to me" does not constitute a speech, and, too often, does not constitute entertainment either. Such stories may serve well as supporting material, but they will not stand alone as the entire speech.

If you began your preparation with the selection of a central theme and formulated a summary statement on that theme, you should have no trouble dividing that statement into its logical component parts. These parts are the major divisions of the body of your speech. There should be only two or three of them, because your entertaining speech should be brief, and each division will have to be supported and illustrated.

After you have organized the major divisions of the body of the speech, being certain that each of the divisions is clearly related to the central theme, you must decide on a conclusion and an introduction for the speech. Both should be brief, but not abrupt. And both should have relevance to the entire theme—not just to the last point or to the first one. Prepare the introduction and conclusion carefully. The introduction sets the mood and the pace for the entire speech, and the conclusion is what your audience will remember longest.

Presentation

Much of the success of the content of the speech to entertain depends on the delivery. Your presentation can either enhance the humor and wit or defeat it. Although each speaker must find the speaking style most suited to himself and adapt that approach to each topic, occasion, and audience, there are some general guidelines on delivery of social speeches.

1. Do not announce your efforts at humor or label your witticisms. To do so is almost to dare your listeners to be amused. If you begin with "This is the funniest story you will ever hear," you are likely to get the response, "I didn't think it was so funny; I expected a great deal more." Take your audience by surprise if you can; it will increase its enjoyment.

2. Watch your audience's response and adapt to it. If your listeners are laughing, do not continue to speak while you cannot be heard, but wait until the laughter has **almost** subsided and then begin again. If your audience is not responding as you had expected, it may be necessary to adapt your speech as you deliver it. If a particular kind of illustration is not successful, you may have to omit another of the same type you had planned to use. Be flexible; be sensitive to your audience's reactions and adjust your speech to them.

3. Keep your own responses to the humor and wit under control. Your purpose is to amuse the **audience,** not to provide a performance

of uncontrolled laughter. If you do laugh at your own comments, keep your chuckles within reasonable bounds; if you respond too much to your own wit, you may find that you are laughing **for** the audience rather than **with** them.

4. Use dialect, if at all, with great restraint. Many groups are understandably sensitive about stereotypes of speech patterns. You may, with the best of motives and without malicious intent, injure feelings or infuriate listeners through the use of dialect. I have found that most dialect stories do not rely for their humor on the dialect anyway; if the story is a genuinely funny one, it will be funny without the brogue. If it is not funny without the unconventional speech pattern, it is likely to be holding a group, a region, or a country up to ridicule—which, I trust, would never be our purpose.

5. The effect of the lines you deliver depends in large part on the timing with which you give them. You must build up to punch lines and present them at the right instant for maximum results. Watch professional comedians and successful speakers; note their use of pause to heighten the impact. Be certain that you do not let the voice fade away or trail off and that you neither mumble the lines nor rattle them off. Punch lines must be given loudly enough to be heard easily, slowly enough to be grasped easily. In short, they must be delivered as a climax; punch lines must be punched! And they must come at the right psychological moment.

6. Bodily activity is as important in the presentation of material to entertain as vocal aspects of delivery. Bodily activity should be controlled and appropriate for your intent and your content. You should give some attention to four aspects of bodily activity: posture, bodily movement, facial expressions, and gestures. Your posture will be determined by the kind of total impression you want to make, the "role" you are playing, the mood of the material you are presenting. Bodily movement should not be aimless motion; you should move your body (including walking to a new position) only for a specific purpose—to mark a transition or to get closer to your audience, for example. Facial expressions should not be overdone; "mugging" can be very distracting. But facial expressions—even grimaces—can contribute to underscore the idea and enhance the humor. Gestures should be meaningful, appropriate, and well-timed; again, they should be in keeping with your purpose, and they should reinforce the ideas rather than detract from them.

Specimen speech

On April 27, 1962, the White House Correspondents and News Photographers Associations held a dinner in the main ballroom of the Sheraton-Park Hotel in Washington. William H. Y. Knighton, Jr., outgoing president of the White House Correspondents Association, presided.

President John F. Kennedy and his guest, Prime Minister Harold Macmillan of Great Britain, were guests at the dinner, as were Vice-President Lyndon B. Johnson and Chief Justice Earl Warren. President Kennedy was asked to make some remarks. It was shortly after his public attack on the steel industry for a price increase, and he surprised and delighted his audience with this parody of his television address on the steel crisis.

Mr. President, Prime Minister, Mr. Vice-President, Mr. Chief Justice, ladies and gentlemen:

I have a few opening announcements. First, the sudden and arbitrary action of the officers of this organization in increasing the price of dinner tickets by $2.50 over last year constitutes a wholly unjustifiable defiance of the public interest. If this increase is not rescinded but is imitated by the gridiron, radio, TV, and other dinners, it will have a serious impact on the entire economy of this city!

In this serious hour in our Nation's history, when newsmen are awakened in the middle of the night to be given a front page story, when expense accounts are being scrutinized by the Congress, when correspondents are required to leave their families for long and lonely weekends at Palm Beach, the American people will find it hard to accept this ruthless decision made by a tiny handful of executives whose only interest is the pursuit of pleasure! I am hopeful that the Women's Press Club will not join this price rise and will thereby force a recision.

I want to congratulate the new officers of the White House Press Correspondents, the old one, Bill Knighton, and Bob Roth. But I must say that I am intrigued by the selection of the photographers. Last year when I came here, the president was Frank Cancellare. And this year it was Arthur Lodovichetti. Next year it's Del Vecchio. I do not want to suggest anything, but I do understand that there was a meeting in upstate New York last night and that next year's president is going to be one of the Muto boys!

I'm sure I speak in behalf of all of us in expressing our thanks and very best wishes to Benny Goodman and his group, Miss Gwen Verdon and Bob Foss, Miss Sally Ann Howes, Mr. Reid—who has some talent—and Mr. Peter

Sellers. I have arranged for them to appear next week on the United States Steel Hour! Actually I didn't do it; Bobby did it!

Like members of Congress, I have been, during the last few days over the Easter holidays, back in touch with my constituents and seeing how they felt. And, frankly, I've come back to Washington from Palm Beach and I'm against my entire program! I really feel that the only hope in '64 is to—on the Republican ticket—is to nominate Barry! But to be honest, I thought that before I went to Palm Beach.

We are glad to have the Prime Minister tonight. Last night he was the guest of the publishers, and again he is tonight. We want him to know how welcome he is. Lord Dunsany, a distinguished Irishman, said many years ago, "To fight England is to fight faith." And I choose to believe in 1962 to be associated with England in a great cause is to be associated with faith.

Prime Minister, we are proud to have you here again. (Applause) And I think I speak on his behalf in saying that after having been in the hands of 1400 members of the press for over 4 hours, we haven't got a single complaint!

Thank you.

Questions for specimen speech analysis

1. Does the speech by President Kennedy reveal careful planning? Was it prepared with that specific audience and occasion in mind? What specific adaptation can be cited?

2. Would this speech contribute to the climate of conviviality and comradeship? Was the speech gracious? Was it in good taste?

3. What was the theme, the central idea, of the speech? Was the topic appropriate for the speaker, audience, and occasion? What element of the familiar did the speech contain? What element of surprise did it contain?

4. Did President Kennedy rely on "canned" humor, or was his humor fresh and original? What "punch lines" can you identify in the speech? Are they funny? Why or Why not?

5. With what kind of wit did the President begin his speech? How was it developed? What other devices did he employ?

6. Did President Kennedy include any non-humorous material? Why? Was it appropriate? Would it destroy the mood of good-fellowship or contribute to it?

7. Did the conclusion establish or clarify the theme and reinforce the mood?

8. Remembering the objectives of the after-dinner speech, how would you rate this speech on over-all effectiveness?

Index